# The Thundering Voice

## "Lessons on Leadership"

## A Moral Approach to Corporate Social Responsibility

Pedro J. Caceres

Strategic Book Publishing
New York, NewYork

Strategic Book Publishing
An imprint of Writers Literary & Publishing Services, Inc.
845 Third Avenue, 6th Floor – 6016
New York, NY 10022
http://www.strategicbookpublishing.com

ISBN: 978-1-60860-134-9, 1-60860-134-X

Printed in the United States of America

Illustrations by Luz Ferez
www.luzferez.com

Book Design/Layout by: Andrew Herzog

I confess to almighty God, and to you, my brothers and sisters, that I have sinned through my own fault, in my thoughts and in my words, in what I have done, and in what I have failed to do; and I ask blessed Mary, ever virgin, all the angels and saints, and you, my brothers and sisters, to pray for me to the Lord our God.

# Dedication

To my loving wife Luz,

To my four princesses

Luz, Arancha, Paloma, and Rocio

# Table of Contents

# Introduction

*September 14, 2008*

I have always held the conviction that business executives have a social responsibility. This thought remained completely unfocused for many years of my professional life. By chance or by fate, one day I decided to buy a small book that I found in a bookshop. The small booklet was *Laborem Exercens,* written by John Paul II. At that time I was already a member of the Corporate Social Responsibility committee for a Fortune 500 company.

That day, my approach to understanding my role as a business manager and leader changed radically. What I read in the book helped me connect my faith to my concern for social issues. I was amazed, and somewhat upset, that having been an active member of a structured body like the Catholic Church for so long, I had come to discover so late the Pope's teachings on social issues.

My immediate reaction was to find out if there was more than *Laborem Exercens* in the teachings of the Catholic faith addressing social questions. My discovery was stunning. I found one of the most amazing documents related to human development in *Populorum Progressio* by Paul VI; I imagined being a worker at the end of the nineteenth century and receiving the gift from God that was *Rerum Novarum*, by Leo XIII.

I couldn't let this happen to other business executives who face the same challenges I have met when trying to align personal faith with business life. I decided to write my doctoral thesis on this subject and, from that research, to write this book on a more personal note, gathering the teachings from the Popes on social and labor issues and sharing them with the world.

It is not my intention to preach to anybody. I am just reproducing literally the Popes' teachings and I am adding comments derived from my professional experience. This is a business book; at its conclusion you will find Appendix G, offering my thoughts on many business issues. I did this to convey my personal approach to the topic of people value and business success.

I do not require the reader to be Catholic or to accept these teachings if their faith leads them on a different path. I am only asking all of you to reflect and draw your own conclusions from what these Holy Fathers of the Catholic Church—also human, and sinners like all of us—came to believe as true.

# Legend

[RN] Encyclical *Rerum Novarum*, on the condition of the working people. Pope Leo XIII (5/15/1891)

[QA] Encyclical *Quadragesimo Anno*, on the fortieth anniversary of *RN*. Pope Pius XI (5/15/1931)

[PP] Encyclical *Populorum Progressio*, on the development of peoples. Pope Paul VI (3/27/1967)

[LE] Encyclical *Laborem Exercens*, on human work. Pope John Paul II (9/14/1981)

[SRS] Encyclical *Sollicitudo Rei Socialis*, on the twentieth anniversary of *PP*. Pope John Paul II (12/31/1987)

[CA] Encyclical *Centesimus Annus*, on the centenary of *Rerun Novarum*. Pope John Paul II (5/1/1991)

# Chapter 1

## *"Blessed are the poor in spirit, for theirs is the kingdom of heaven."*

I have been a member of the Corporate Social Responsibility Committee for two different Fortune 500 companies. In my role as operations executive, I have managed thousands of people in the global marketplace and have come to realize that companies succeed if they have a vision, a lot of passion and energy, and the right combination of people, process, and technology. Success certainly doesn't happen spontaneously.

I have also learned throughout my career that machines, facilities, operating procedures, and the like are merely enabling technologies. They don't have passion. They don't have a soul. It is only the willingness of a human who says "I can and I will" that creates the force and momentum necessary to move mountains. Only people who align their own interests with the interests of the team can make or break the performance of any company.

Many discussions are currently taking place regarding Corporate Social Responsibility and the environment. These are legitimate concerns, but this emphasis on the environment makes me very uneasy. I can't help thinking all the time that, at the heart of all this, there are *people* who bear the consequences of companies' behavior. For me, the human development aspect of Corporate Social Responsibility is being sorely undervalued.

Corporate Social Responsibility (CSR) is becoming an intrinsic component of every company's way of doing business. It arose as a reaction by the business community to many cases of questionable executive behavior, more demanding consumers who are quite aware of sustainability issues and climate change, a broader global market, and the push for human rights from many different organizations. Like many other business-related initiatives, the emphasis on CSR has grown because it actually delivered on its promise of helping many corporations grow and, simultaneously, increase their operational performance.

Corporate Social Responsibility (CSR) is a concept whereby organizations consider the interests of society in all aspects of their operations, by taking responsibility for the impact of their activities on customers, employees, shareholders, communities, and the environment. This obligation is understood to extend beyond the statutory obligation to comply with legislation; organizations voluntarily take further steps to improve the quality of life for employees and their families, as well as for the local community and society at large.

The reason this happens is the unique way that CSR addresses the social concerns of all stakeholders:

- Customers who want to know that they are buying products that are environmentally friendly, from companies that are committed to their community;

- Employees who want to work for companies that really care about their health and safety and don't discriminate;

- Shareholders who want to make sure that the companies they are investing in can guarantee a future return, and which have a good management team;

- Governments that want to promote growth that is sustainable and supportive of their social policies.

CSR is being integrated into the strategic process of companies. In most cases, it has become the foundation of corporate strategy itself.

A simple way to represent this is with a pyramid where the Foundation is the CSR framework, on which is built strategic Planning, Values, and, ultimately, the Vision of the company.

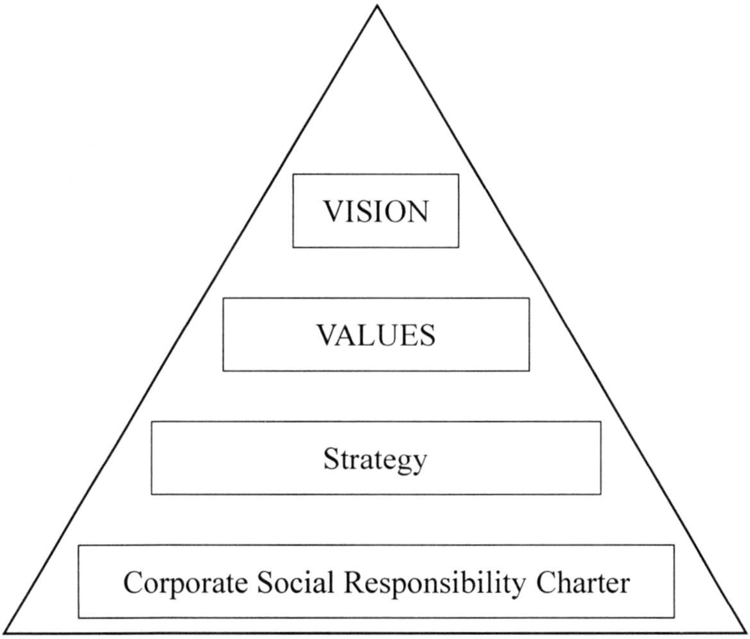


Companies know that this pyramid will drive their behavior in the marketplace and will shape roles and responsibilities, policies, processes, and procedures. This pyramid will also define how the company interacts with individuals, communities, and markets. "At Gap Inc., social responsibility is fundamental to who we are and how we operate as a company" (www.gapinc.com).

Companies are sharing this charter and their CSR performance with the entire world. Many of them publish annual reports stating where they stand in all aspects of their Social Responsibility Charter. On the other hand, companies that do not are perceived to be more open to the risk of endangering future performance, and they end up paying a penalty in the eyes of the investor community.

It is my belief that Corporate Social Responsibility is to companies what social responsibility is to people. Following this logic, both humans and corporations need a comprehensive and solid set of rules that, respecting their individual freedom, provide a way to make things right for all their stakeholders.

They both need a moral foundation that addresses *human development*: "Freedom from misery, the greater assurance of finding subsistence, health and fixed employment; an increased share of responsibility without oppression of any kind and in security from situations that do violence to their dignity as men; better education" [PP-6].

When analyzing Corporate Social Responsibility charters, it becomes very evident that they are all quite similar in nature. They differ in the number of stated values they declare, the priorities they give to different aspects of the charter, and their specific goals, but in the end, there is no significant difference, and rightly so: as mentioned before, from the stakeholder's perspective, one wants to see the same level of CSR commitment from all companies with which one is involved.

The core aspects of any CSR statement are usually based on the following ideas:

- Human development and the recognition of human dignity

- Employees as the most important asset of an enterprise

- Contribution, solidarity, and community development
- Sustainability and a concern for the environment
- The need for transparent corporate governance
- The need to recognize profitability as a tool for society's advancement.

This core set of considerations is not different from the list of moral and social issues men face in the world of economics. The scope of this list is very broad and the laws of economics are driving companies to address some of these issues with far more energy and resources than they address others: in today's world, the issue of sustainability and the concern for the environment is taking priority over the rest of the concerns on the list.

CSR is not enjoying a free ride, anyway. Many companies are developing the concept out of a fear of being left out of current business trends. These companies have not yet internalized the real meaning of CSR and, of course, are more worried about their public image and formalities than the actual benefits that CSR can offer.

Of course, there is a context for everything, and in this day and age it is very clear that many economic systems and companies follow the teachings of Milton Friedman, whose central belief was that "the business of business is business": the only goal of business is to maximize shareholders' value; anything else is socialism. This idea has shaped the Western world of economics, with its main exponent being the USA model. For these scholars and business executives, and there are many, Corporate Social Responsibility is an invention lacking demonstrable business value. Nonetheless, they are willing to play the CSR "game," superficially perhaps, yet still socially respectable.

It is clear that, even if one doesn't realize it, there is a moral implication to such ideas: the belief that the end justifies the means, the world is for the fittest, and an eye for an eye or (as sometimes happens) a thousand eyes for an eye. These "laws of the jungle" are the same beliefs that today are fueling the gospel of wealth in the Christian world, and the individualist approach to life and society. So it is very inaccurate to think that men can separate their spiritual beliefs from their human behavior. Even if they believe that the separation of spiritual from material life is possible, by negating the fact of that connection, they are actually maintaining a dialog with their spiritual being.

The people who seem to be moving the wires of the economy and enjoying great success are setting an example for those who want to realize their own business or personal success; they become role models. The problem is that these individuals, for the most part, follow the same three laws of the jungle I mentioned earlier, so the system perpetuates. There is a very clear distinction for me between the spirituality that emanates from the values of love, mercy, and hope and other spiritual values. I am not talking about right and wrong; I am talking about what is allowed or not allowed to followers of certain religions. People who are honest with their spirituality will behave according to those rules. If the rules let them take financial advantage of the meek, they will do it and they won't feel guilty. For them, it would be okay to look for wealth with no regard to their neighbor's welfare.

I think the current world of economics is managed by the group of individuals I just mentioned. They experience no guilt; they exercise no restraint when seeking individual success and limitless wealth. Individual success, no matter what, is proof that their life is successful. *Wrong.*

I will maintain throughout this book the idea that Corporate Social Responsibility is a subset of a larger moral doctrine, and that the values, culture, behavior, and social responsibility charter of any corporation reflects the prevailing moral beliefs of any given society. I also maintain that the evolution of a CSR charter, if it is expected to achieve any future success, will follow a path toward integral human development.

I conducted a comparison between the CSR concept and the comprehensive social doctrine of the Catholic Church covering all aspects of integral human development and its relationship to work and the economy. It must be obvious by now that my heritage and life experience is immersed in the Catholic faith. I ask people of different faiths to read this book without prejudice. I am sure it will provoke good intellectual discussions that will help all individuals to move a step forward in their own human development.

I called this book *The Thundering Voice* based on Pope Pius IX's comments when talking about the first document ever published by the Catholic Church regarding the "social question." That document was the encyclical *Rerum Novarum,* on the condition of the working people, released by Pope Leo XIII in 1891; Pius declares that "The Apostolic voice did not thunder forth in vain" [QA-12].

It is shocking that the first-ever published document regarding the social question was issued in almost the twentieth century, but it is more shocking that this document and all the subsequent documents released by the Popes to light the way for Catholics and humankind in general concerned with human development have been generally ignored. How many executives, or even the general populace, have ever read any of the documents published by the Church in this past century?

I have been a practitioner of my faith for all my life and I have been a business executive for almost twenty years; I have faced many situations and questions that needed a better moral foundation, a more pragmatic foundation. I came in contact with the encyclical *Laborem Exercens* (on human work) released by John Paul II in 1981 when I was traveling on one of many business trips. I opened it and read a shocking statement regarding labor relations. I couldn't believe that the Pope would actually address those issues, never mind the social question.

I started reading the entire encyclical and it opened before me an incredible world of teachings, reflections, frustrations, and calls for action as I have never seen before. I imagined the Pope sitting at his desk writing about the issues that I was confronting every day in my working life, and helping me find the answers to all my questions. I read his firmly-stated thoughts that challenged my relativism. I felt guilty of ignoring the basics of the connection of my faith to my working life and to the development of people, and I felt happy realizing that my approach to business had a social component that was rooted in my very own faith and aligned with the teachings of the Popes.

I felt the emptiness of my spirit. How poor I was!

I couldn't stop with *Laborem Exercens*. I printed out all the encyclicals that had to do with the social question. I read them all. I broke them down into pieces. I even created a database. I classified all the topics; I looked for the main themes. It was just an amazing experience. What a remarkable set of teachings!

One after another, I read and analyzed the following documents published by the Popes of the Catholic Church:

- Encyclical *Rerum Novarum* [RN], on the condition of the working people. Pope Leo XIII (5/15/1891)

- Encyclical *Quadragesimo Anno* [QA], on the fortieth anniversary of *RN*. Pope Pius XI (5/15/1931)

- Pastoral Constitution *Gaudium et Spes* [Happiness and Hope], on the Church in the modern world. Pope Paul VI (12/7/1965)

- Encyclical *Populorum Progressio* [PP], on the development of peoples. Pope Paul VI (3/27/1967)

- Encyclical *Laborem Exercens* [LE], on human work. Pope John Paul II (9/14/1981)

- Encyclical *Sollicitudo Rei Socialis* [SRS], on the twentieth anniversary of *Populorum Progressio*. Pope John Paul II (12/31/1987)

- Encyclical *Centesimus Annus* [CA], on the centenary of *Rerun Novarum*. Pope John Paul II (5/1/1991)

I also analyzed the magnificent *Compendium of the Social Doctrine of the Church*, published on April 2, 2004 by the Pontifical Council for Justice and Peace, which contains an analysis of all social documents ever published by the Holy See.

All these documents, when read with intention and purpose, are incredible testaments of the beliefs of the successors of Christ regarding men and their contribution to God's creation and human development. I realized that what I really wanted was to share my experience with all the people, so I decided to write *The Thundering Voice*.

In the basic foundation of all I learned is the following statement: "For the Catholic Church the salvation is salvation for all people and of the whole person; it is universal and integral salvation. It concerns the human person in all his dimensions: personal and social, spiritual and corporeal, historical and transcendent" (*Compendium of the Social Doctrine of the Church*).

From the *Compendium*, we learn that the permanent principles of the Church's social doctrine constitute the very heart of Catholic social teaching. These are the principles of:

- The dignity of the human person, which is the foundation of all the other principles and content of the Church's social doctrine.

- The common good—to which every aspect of social life must be related if it is to attain its fullest meaning—stems from the dignity, unity, and equality of all people.

- Subsidiarity, by which all societies of a superior order must adopt attitudes of help ("subsidium")—therefore, of support, promotion, development—with respect to lower-order societies.

- Solidarity, which highlights in a particular way the intrinsically social nature of the human person, the equality of all in dignity and rights, and the common path of individuals and peoples toward an ever more-committed unity.

The characteristics shared by CSR and the social doctrine of the Church, and the many examples of actual business issues that I have confronted where CSR came up short of answers, motivated me to look for an expansion of the CSR framework that was suggested by the *Compendium*; I sought to created a model that is complete, comprehensive, robust, and logically sound.

The Church has carried forward the mission and the Popes, Christ's representatives on earth elected through the inspiration of the Holy Spirit, have intervened and adapted Christ's doctrine to provide light to men according to the needs of their times. "It must not be forgotten that the passing of time and the changing of social circumstances will require a constant updating of the reflections on the various issues raised here, in order to interpret the new signs of the times" (*Compendium of Social Doctrine of the Catholic Church*).

The Popes wrote letters to the universal Church and to all men of good will addressing many issues that concerned them at different stages of their tenure. Some of those letters, called encyclicals, dealt front and center with the "social question."

"Following on the Second Vatican Ecumenical Council a renewed consciousness of the demands of the Gospel makes it [the Church's] duty to put herself at the service of all, to help them grasp their serious problem in all its dimensions, and to convince them that solidarity in action at this turning point in human history is a matter of urgency" [PP-1].

Man decided to part ways with his spiritual being during the Renaissance by splitting human nature into two different components: the spiritual aspect, understood as a mystic connection to God; and the material one that deals with the world, social issues, and whatever earthly matters affect men.

Why men separated material from spiritual can only be answered by recognizing that there is a natural human tendency to avoid suffering, compromise, and responsibility and, through that separation, men could pursue a materialistic life, reaching to the spiritual side to thank God for riches, or complain about miseries or, most of the time, to fulfill certain traditions.

The crisis initiated by the separation of body and soul opened again the possibility of rejoining them even better than before. This will certainly require a new vision based on the idea that all men are created equal, have equal rights, and must share the responsibility to continue God's creation.

In the Middle Ages, Christianity was the religion of the state; religious authority and political power were too closely intertwined, and the most important attribute of man, his freedom of choice, was impaired. This is still happening in many countries and many religions. Fundamentalism has become a strong force supporting regimes that lack respect for human rights. Fundamentalism and anarchy are two faces of the same coin, the coin of lack of human development.

In today's world, men with solid moral background and an unquestionable respect for human rights are looking at the world differently. Men, as actors of the creation and agents of development, have the responsibility to promote the ethical behavior that eventually will constitute the foundation for Corporate Social Responsibility. "The joys and the hopes, the grieves and the anxieties of the men of this age, especially those who are poor or in any way afflicted, these are the joys and hopes, the grieves and anxieties of the followers of Christ" (Paul VI, *Gaudium et Spes*).

For true Christians, free men recognize the role of Christ in their lives, freely accepting the responsibility of carrying out His teachings, coming together and leading the transformation of society into something that pleases God. That will be the end result of God's plan for humanity: all men sharing in the riches of the universe created by God with "freedom from misery; the greater assurance of finding subsistence, health, and fixed employment; an increased share of responsibility without oppression of any kind and in security from situations that do violence to their dignity as men; better education" [PP-6].

The world is not addressing the need of material development and spiritual development synchronously or effectively: "There is also the scandal of glaring inequalities not merely in the enjoyment of possessions but even more in the exercise of power. While a small restricted group enjoys a refined civilization in certain regions, the remainder of the population, poor and scattered, is deprived of nearly all possibility of personal initiative and of responsibility, and oftentimes even its living and working conditions are unworthy of the human person…At the same time social conflicts have taken on world dimensions" [PP-9].

"It remains only too true that the resultant situation is manifestly inadequate for facing the hard reality of modern economics" [PP-8]. "The earth, even though apportioned among private owners, ceases not thereby to minister to the needs of all, inasmuch as there is not one who does not sustain life from what the land produces. Those who do not possess the soil contribute their labor; hence, it may truly be said that all human subsistence is derived either from labor on one's own land, or from some toil, some calling, which is paid for either in the produce of the land itself, or in that which is exchanged for what the land brings forth" [RN-8], but "rich peoples enjoy rapid growth whereas the poor develop slowly. The imbalance is on the increase: some produce a surplus of foodstuffs, others cruelly lack them and see their exports made uncertain" [PP-8].

This imbalance of rich and poor has always concerned the spiritual side of men while the material one kept going in the wrong direction: "The same feeling those many Catholics, both priests and laymen, shared, whom a truly wonderful charity had long spurred on to relieve the unmerited poverty of the non-owning workers, and who could in no way convince themselves that so enormous and unjust an inequality in the distribution of this world's goods truly conforms to the designs of the all-wise Creator" [QA-5].

The Popes of the Church have spoken like a thundering voice: "The Apostolic voice did not thunder forth in vain," affirms Pope Pius XI [QA-12] when writing about Leo XIII's *Rerum Novarum*. These encyclicals, from the *Rerum Novarum* to John Paul II's *Centesimus Annus*, are incredible documents that can't be ignored any longer by Catholics or any other people of good will.

# Chapter 2

## *"Blessed are they who mourn, for they shall be comforted."*

John XXIII teaches us that it is a reality that all human beings could have enough to eat, basic education, and basic health if men would just start following God's will; this teaching is important and its application urgent. "Today the peoples in hunger are making a dramatic appeal to the peoples blessed with abundance" [PP-3].

There are many resources in the world used for man's evil actions. It is technically demonstrable that only a fraction of those resources would be enough to change the balance of misery and poverty in the world. Many people mourn unnecessarily.

The gross domestic product (GDP) of each of the world's nations as of 2006 totaled $66 trillion (Central Intelligence Agency's *The World Fact Book 2006*), of which Europe represented 20 percent and the US 20 percent, China/Japan/India almost 30 percent, and the rest of the world the remaining 30 percent.

Let's try to come up with an estimated figure for the money that annually goes into wars, the armament race, drugs, ecological destruction, and all other inventions of human evil (or protection against it). If we assume that number to be (a low) 3 percent of the world's totaled GDP, the cost of evildoing and defense against it would be about $2 trillion.

It's astonishing that we need to combine the purchasing power of two-thirds of the countries of the world to get that amount of money.

Another cancer on our economic system is the financial speculation that attaches artificial values to good and services without any connection to their value-adding activity. Financial speculation involves the buying, holding, selling, and short-selling of stocks, bonds, commodities, currencies, collectibles, real estate, derivatives, or any valuable financial instrument to profit from fluctuations in its price, as opposed to buying it for use or for income such as from dividends or interest.

Why do I believe that financial speculation has a devastating, negative effect on people's development? First, let me say that I am not the only one: in his message on World Peace Day (January 1, 2009) Pope Benedict XVI blamed financial speculation for poverty and called for a "common code of ethics" to stabilize the increasingly globalized economy.

He characterized the global financial system as "self-centered, short-sighted, and lacking in concern for the poor." He could probably say it louder but not clearer. On the other hand, we know about the ban on short-selling imposed by many central securities agencies worldwide to mitigate the effects of the September 2008 financial meltdown. Some governments have gone even further lately, with bills directed to impose taxes on oil speculation which has been blamed for 75 percent of the oil price increase that happened during the first half of 2008.

The amount of speculative wealth being generated is not reaching a wide population of individuals and societies. An astonishing $29 billion generated by hedge funds in 2008 went to only fifty individuals. These hedge funds gambled heavily in the commodity and metal sectors, ultimately impoverishing an undetermined number of people globally, surely in the millions.

The University of Santa Cruz published a report called "Who Rules America?", which states that as of 1999, the top 1 percent of the populace owned almost 40 percent of the wealth in America. Since the 1980s, the share of income from capital gains going to the top 1 percent of American has been increasing. Today 57.5 percent of capital gains income goes to the richest 1 percent of Americans.

I am going to state something that, to me, is very obvious: taxes should be shifted away from productive activity onto unproductive activity. Capital gains should be taxed at least as much as ordinary income. Currency speculation should be taxed.

The graph below shows the share of capital income received by the top 1 percent and bottom 80 percent of Americans from 1979 to 2003.

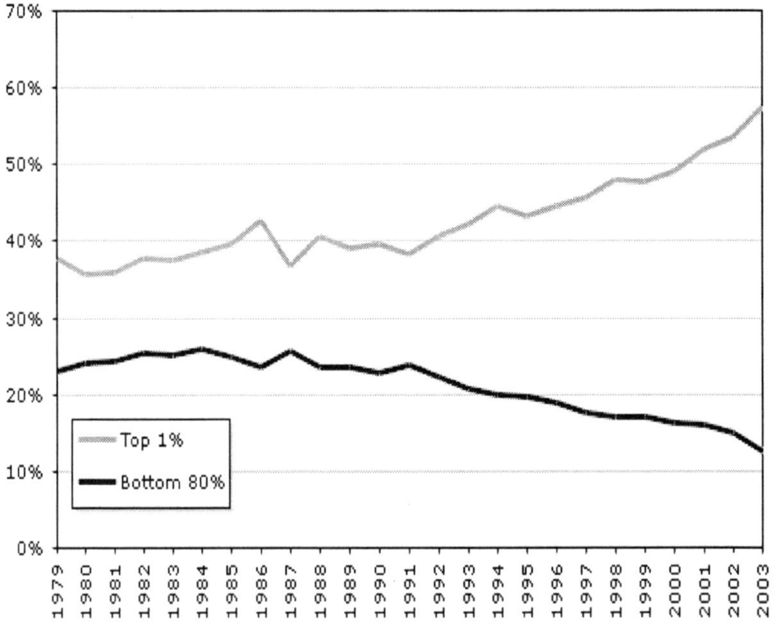

The Global Policy Forum released a document in the year 2000 where the issue of taxing non-value-adding activities was addressed by very specific proposals:

*"By taxing financial speculation, trading in stocks, bonds, futures, options, foreign currencies, and other financial instruments, it would be possible to have either a large reduction in tax rates for a typical working family, or to provide for many of the nation's unmet social needs. A small tax on financial speculation, such as a 0.25 percent tax on the sale or purchase of a share of stock, would have very little impact on people who buy these assets as an investment to hold. The bulk of this tax would be paid by people who speculate in financial assets, often buying and selling them in the same day. Such speculation is soaring as new technology allows round the clock trading over the Internet. Such speculation is really just a form of gambling, and deserves to be treated like gambling."*

For the Catholic Church, "Experienced in human affairs, the Church, without attempting to interfere in any way in the politics of States, seeks but a solitary goal: to carry forward the work of Christ Himself under the lead of the befriending Spirit...Sharing the noblest aspirations of men and suffering when she sees them not satisfied, she wishes to help them attain their full flowering, and that is why she offers men what she possesses as her characteristic attribute: a global vision of man and of the human race" [PP-13]. As John Paul II affirms in *Centesimus Annus* [55]: "The theological dimension is needed both for interpreting and for solving present-day problems in human society."

Pope Benedict XVI made a devastating comment regarding the financial system during the 2009 World Peace Day address: "It is because of this [speculation], he added, that finance has lost its role as a bridge between the present and the future, in the creation of new production opportunities, and employment in the long term."

This crisis didn't start as an industrial crisis, an oil crisis, or even a commodity crisis. This crisis is the product of two super bubbles that were connected: the first super bubble tied to real estate speculation and a second super bubble tied to derivative products supported by the first bubble. It was like building a house of cards on top of a huge house of cards. Both went down fast and furious.

We have to admit that we are all responsible for the first super bubble, the real estate frenzy—we all like to see our properties gain value, and we got carried away. And then the banks followed: investment banks first, commercial banks later, insurance companies, and so forth. They added salt to wounds and they killed the system. I am not sure if we can say that there are financial investment banks per se in the US any longer; the two institutions that survived were allowed to transform themselves into commercial banks.

I can't believe that all the executives of those companies were stupid. Some of the companies had been operating for more than a century. So what happened? I think the answer is that they gambled with no restraints and they lost. They gambled billions of dollars and were immensely compensated while the game was still going. And one day, in some cases literally in one day, they lost everything.

I am certain that all these companies had a Corporate Social Responsibility charter and I am even more certain that it didn't work to protect their companies, employees, or shareholders from the debacle.

I invite you to read the Social Funds report on Lehman Brothers at http://www.socialfunds.com. You probably wouldn't have hesitated to invest in a company with that profile. I also invite you to read the incredible report on environmental sustainability released by Lehman Brothers in 2007. This same company bought a stake in the SkyPower company of Canada, and was praised for all their contributions to climate change control and environmental sustainability.

I am not picking on Lehman Brothers. They happened to fail on September 15, 2008, which will probably go down in history as the first day of the second Great Depression. I could say the same thing about many other companies, all of them with great Corporate Social Responsibility charters, great environmental policies, great concern for diversity, great everything. They had it all to succeed, and they failed.

This should be enough argument to support the idea that Corporate Social Responsibility is not enough to guarantee business success. CSR comes up short on delivering a sustainable long term business model. CSR lacks the moral and behavioral foundation to secure businesses against greed, speculation, and all economic sins.

This is the major difference between CSR and the social doctrine of the Catholic Church, between a materialistic and a spiritual approach to life.

I do not maintain that the Catholic Church is the only organized entity that can substantiate a Corporate Social Responsibility model. The precepts of any other moral body, religious or non-religious, that connects the material and spiritual components of the human being could be used as the basis of a Corporate Social Responsibility charter. The resulting program would be distinguished by the premises and arguments from that body's specific moral code.

For some religions, the call for struggle against democratic ideas will result in a set of values that are radically different from Christian values. Some fundamentalist societies could develop business values completely unacceptable to other societies. Western companies share a common understanding of what constitutes social responsibility; these shared assumptions can differ from another culture's point of view. I affirm that the values, behavior, and social responsibility charter of any corporation reflects the moral beliefs of any given society.

This can be understood from the standpoint of every company's need to brand its products and create an emotional connection with its customers, wherever they are. This is precisely one of the aspects that make globalization a complex adventure. To connect with customers on a global basis, companies either have to reach the common moral background of all those different cultures or localize their message and behavior.

This is one of the reasons companies have to balance the request from their stakeholders to do something about environment, education, poverty, etc. against requests from the governments in the countries where they operate to refrain from disseminating ideas contrary to their local political interests.

In this global economy, no business can succeed without addressing the question of what their values are, what their image is, and how they are going to act regarding sustainable growth and human development.

The field of Corporate Social Responsibility is extensive and its range is actually still expanding. I decided to limit the scope of this book to the main aspects of Corporate Social Responsibility that affect the management of companies for profit in the present world. The topics that I will cover in the book are the following:

**Ethical behavior**

- The concept of property

- The balanced approach to profitability

- Globalization

- Ethical consumerism
- Fiscal responsibility
- Work compensation

**Sustainability**

- Sustainable development
- Climate change
- Energy conservation

**The People Value**

- Work environment, respect, and dignity
- Diversity
- Education
- Employee participation

**Human Development**

- Individual
- Family
- Community
- The global village
- The passion for excellence

# Chapter 3

## *"Blessed are the meek, for they shall inherit the earth."*

In this chapter we will learn about the different theories that form the basis of Corporate Social Responsibility. The concept of social responsibility is so critical to the guaranteed future performance of a corporation that I wanted to go beyond what has already been written and find the foundation of all those strategies that are now being implemented, understand how they connect with each other, and predict the evolution of CSR policies. And it is very evident that what the CSR charters are looking for now is for a complete answer to the question: How can corporations participate actively and lead the real integral development of men as members of society and invaluable assets of any company?

The field of Corporate Social Responsibility has been the subject of many papers and it has clearly reached a high level of development in recent years. There are many concepts related to this topic and we can find those under any of the following headings:

*Accountability, Business in the community, Business ethics, Business philosophy, Civil society, Corporate behavior, Corporate benefit, Corporate governance, Corporate sustainability, Corporate personhood, Customer engagement, Ethicism, Ethical banking, Ethical consumerism, Global Reporting Initiative, Inclusive business, Not Just For Profit, OECD Guidelines for Multinational*

*Enterprises, Socially responsible investing, Sustainability, United Nations Global Compact, Voluntary compliance...*

As mentioned earlier in the book, I have been part of one Corporate Social Responsibility committee for a Fortune 500 company and also member of a Corporate Sustainability Steering Committee for a different Fortune 500 company. In both cases I have participated in corporate policy-making, training and communications, and project implementation.

CSR charters address the following four groups of issues:

- Social issues affecting the corporation (diversity and inclusion, health and safety)

- Environmental issues (climate change and energy, efficient use of resources and sustainability)

- Product stewardship (green materials, packaging, recycling policies)

- Governance (strategy, communication and reporting, training)

My favorite, by far, is the social aspect, followed by the environmental issues. I understand the importance of the four and I applaud when a corporation is able to address the four of them in a strongly interconnected way.

The governance aspect of the CSR is probably the single most important change in corporate culture. Most cases of erratic corporate behavior in the financial world happen in companies that have a very well-structured CSR but did not have strong governance policy, processes, or procedures.

Sarbanes-Oxley legislation came to close the loophole of wrongful, unethical, and sometimes illegal operational business practices, to prevent cases like Enron. The issue of the current recession has its root in speculative, high-risk, and sometimes illegal financial practices and financial greed. There was no shield for those practices; they should have been picked up by board governance. Some banks said No to the high-risk practices of subprime loans and derivatives and are still running strong. Some others fell into the trap and have paid, and are paying, for this mistake. (I should probably say "are causing all of us to pay" for them.)

What aspects of governance could have been useful to avoid the present crisis? Let us first understand the concept of Corporate Governance as defined by the Organisation for Economic Cooperation and Development: "Corporate governance is the system by which business corporations are directed and controlled. The corporate governance structure specifies the distribution of rights and responsibilities among different participants in the corporation, such as, the board, managers, shareholders and other stakeholders, and spells out the rules and procedures for making decisions on corporate affairs. By doing this, it also provides the structure through which the company objectives are set, and the means of attaining those objectives and monitoring performance" (OECD, April 1999).

For a snapshot, we could simplify by citing J. Wolfensohn, president of the Word Bank, as quoted in an article in *Financial Times*, June 21, 1999: "Corporate governance is about promoting corporate fairness, transparency and accountability."

Just by reading these definitions it is clear that the issue of transparency was for years considered crucial, and still is. The main issue of today's financial crisis is that nobody can put a number on how much banks have and how much they owe. They have not even yet, as of today, disclosed the obligations they took in derivative and future markets that have, in a blink of an eye, lost their value. I have the feeling that it doesn't matter how much money we put into these institutions—they don't know where the bottom is, and that is the reason why the credit crunch is still killing so many innocent people. The banks need the money for themselves! To write off toxic assets that they know are not worth what they have on their books. A simple suggestion would be to have the government force a once-off write down of a significant percentage of bank assets and force their shareholders to bear the cost through the elimination of dividends and the restructuring of managers' compensation with stronger emphasis in sustainable long term financial stability and business growth.

Because no institutions—nor the regulators—disclosed these risky practices in this "Ponzi" scheme, there was no transparency or fairness and all investments were made into a corrupted system. The checks and balances in the system disappeared once the barrier to the merging of stockbrokers, banks, and insurance companies was lifted by legislation like the Commodity Futures Modernization Act of 2000 and the Gramm-Leach-Bliley Act of 1999.

So no transparency and, worst of all, no accountability. In any enterprise the responsibility and accountability starts with the board of directors. As can be read on Microsoft's Web site: "*Strong corporate governance at Microsoft starts with a Board of Directors that is independent, engaged, committed, and effective. Our Board establishes, maintains, and monitors standards and policies for ethics, business practices, and compliance that span the company. Working with management, we set strategic business objectives, ensure that Microsoft has leadership that is dynamic and responsive, track performance, and institute strong financial controls. We believe in strengthening investor confidence and creating long-term shareholder value so we can continue to deliver technology innovations that provide opportunities for customers and for Microsoft.*"

If the board of directors of any institution does not exercise its rights to challenge management and establish strong checks and balances, the likelihood of erratic company behavior is high when compared to companies where the board of directors assume responsibility and feel individually accountable.

In an article in the *Wall Street Journal* on September 15, 2008, Dennis K. Berman shares his thoughts on this issue:

"As the world nervously awaits the effects of the unprecedented Lehman Brothers liquidation, one can't help but wonder how and why this board let its long-time chairman and patron, Richard Fuld, Jr., cling to both hope and power.

Perhaps it was because Mr. Fuld wanted it that way. Over the years, Mr. Fuld had become the living embodiment of that securities firm, creating a top-down culture that sometimes had a military feel to it. Most mornings, Mr. Fuld rode alone in an elevator up to his executive suite. His colleagues simply call him 'The Chairman.' And it is telling that press accounts of Lehman's capital-raising efforts focused entirely on the efforts of Mr. Fuld, and make nary a mention of the ten other members of Lehman's board.

Who was on this board? Until the 2008 arrival of former US Bancorp chief Jerry Grundhofer, the group was lacking in current financial-knowledge firepower. A number of the members did have past financial-markets expertise, but most of their working lives were tied to a different era—the one before massive securitization, credit-default swaps, derivatives trading, and all the risks those products created."

I wonder what kind of accountability this board could exercise over the CEO. In the end, companies get what they deserve. If shareholders don't engage in real company steering, failing to select appropriate members for the board; if the boards don't follow through on their fiduciary responsibility; if corporate management don't have a strong CSR approach, the results can be predicted. I don't know why we are surprised now. What else could happen?

In an article from *Business Respect* (issue number 51, dated March 9, 2003), Alice and John Tepper Marlin offered their description of the evolution of Corporate Social Responsibility. They differentiated three phases:

**Phase I** - The first phase of CSR reporting consisted of advertisements and annual report sections in the 1970s and 1980s that paid homage to the environment. There were a few isolated corporate efforts, such as that by Abbot & Associates in 1972, to add an environmental report to its annual financial statements but it was strictly related to air and water pollution; its financial auditor disclaimed any responsibility for the data on the basis that no standards had been introduced for such audits. It also rashly attempted to reduce everything to a dollar-value bottom line.

**Phase II** - The second phase of CSR reporting, of which the Body Shop and Shell Canada are examples, really began with Ben & Jerry's, which in 1989 commissioned a "social auditor" to work with the B&J staff on a report covering 1988. This social auditor recommended that the report be called a "Stakeholders Report" (the concept of "stakeholders" existed, but this was possibly the first-ever report addressed to stakeholders as such) and that it be divided into the major stakeholder categories: Communities (Community Outreach, Philanthropic Giving, Environmental Awareness, and Global Awareness), Employees, Customers, Suppliers, and Investors.

**Phase III** - The third phase of CSR reporting introduces not only third-party certification of the reports, but certification by bodies that are accredited to certify using social or environmental standards. The standards are already determined before an auditor goes in and the procedures specified. When a violation is found, the facility is given a chance to take corrective action. Some of the violations are considered small, some are serious enough to put certification in jeopardy; the auditor determines, and later returns to see that required corrective actions are made. Major problems are not allowed to remain year after year. The global leader of the new phase in the social area is Social Accountability International (SAI), founded in 1997. The first facility certified against its multi-stakeholder global standard was an Avon factory in New York State, on January 1, 1998. Other pioneers on the environmental side were the Forest Stewardship Council, the International Federation of Organic Agriculture, and the Dutch Max Havelaar Foundation (now FairTrade).

In all cases, every phase was initiated by a company assuming a leadership role in developing innovative new approaches to the same problem: the need to deliver short term results compatible with sustainable long term growth.

What will be the fourth phase in CSR? I believe that the next phase will target the core of CSR, human development, which will be a response to the following challenges:

- The widening gap between rich and poor people
- The widening gap between rich and poor societies
- The growth of underdeveloped communities within developed countries
- The issue of immigration
- The global challenge of fundamentalism and terrorism
- The certain death of individualism
- The spread of social and spiritual relativism
- The inability of governments to provide human and social development

The tension among all these groups can be minimized only by an incredible push for human development, and again, business will have to step up and lead the transformation. They will act as supra-national entities with global reach, that can provide the vision, will, and means to lead the change.

In his paper published in November of 2005 on the Jus Semper Global Alliance Web site, titled "The Future of CSR Will Mirror the Health of Society: Pondering the Evolution of CSR," Álvaro de Regil Castilla affirms that "given the pressing social and environmental decay, society will not allow the current ethos to prevail, and it is already seeking to build an ethos of real and direct democracy, participative and bottom up, that places social welfare above the private interest. In this way, the future of CSR, as such, will disappear to assimilate itself to the paradigmatic shift in which social welfare becomes the primary purpose of business, governed by universal laws and standards that rule its activity."

This regulation must be self-imposed by businesses if they want to have a controlled outcome.

De Regil Castilla also states that the failure of the current system will be the fault of current business practices: "The motive is the maximum flexibility of the factors of production, in such a way that the owners of capital can freely exercise their creative and Darwinian destruction by moving in pursuit of the best locations to produce, to have access to the most efficient labor markets and to have access to consumer markets. The so-called neoliberal globalization means that consumer markets, production and labor have been globalized, by opening the economies of nations to global corporations for their free access in the way it best fits them. But wages and a universal welfare system have not been globalized. Thus, corporations roam the world in search of the most convenient and friendly locations for production and the exploitation of human and natural resources without a global framework imposing a set of responsibilities in order to achieve a sustainable market system. The supply side has been globalized with all its inherent benefits for the industrialists, but the demand side premeditatedly has not, with all the inherent harm to societies and the environment. To maximize shareholder value is the sole objective."

Allen White, in his article "Fade, Integrate or Transform? The Future of CSR" on the Web site of Business for Social Responsibility, describes three potential future scenarios for CSR:

1. **"Fad-and-Fade scenario."** White depicts this scenario, under a severe economic global crisis, where "CSR, once viewed as irreversibly destined to become integral to corporate strategy, management and governance, has proven to be fragile and transient. Attention of business and government turns to basic economic survival and recovery from the crisis. CSR moves quietly into hibernation with an uncertain future, characterized by practices associated with its earliest phase, namely compliance and philanthropy."

2. "**Embed-and-integrate scenario."** This scenario is depicted as the triumph of the CSR movement, for companies have moved to embed CSR as a core part of corporate strategy and operations. As White asserts, "For large and small, public and private companies alike, CSR is the rule; the small fraction of firms that fail to grasp this find themselves increasingly at a competitive disadvantage."

3. "**Transition-and-transformation scenario."** White foresees the transformation of CSR into a broader framework of self-accountability and regulation that will support the case for human development. He envisions these principles as a concept that strives to foster the innovation and competitive instincts of companies while elevating social purpose as the preeminent goal of the corporation:

1. The purpose of the corporation is to harness private interests in service to the public interest.

2. Corporations shall accrue fair returns for shareholders, but not at the expense of the legitimate interests of other stakeholders.

3. Corporations shall operate sustainably, meeting the needs of the present generation without compromising the ability of future generations to meet their needs.

4. Corporations shall distribute their wealth equitably among those who contribute to its creation.

5. Corporations shall be governed in a manner that is participatory, transparent, ethical and accountable.

6. Corporate rights shall not infringe on the right of natural persons to govern themselves, nor infringe on other universal human rights.

The truth is that the future of CSR depends on its ability to deliver on its promises, to provide a balance between short term profits and sustainable long term growth. Is it too late for CSR to really make a difference? The speed of the changes taking place in CSR is encouraging. If this is happening it is because people in developed countries have adopted the sense of urgency that is needed to trigger change. CSR can fail if this speed of change toward human development is not fast enough to catch up with past practices and problems.

And mainly it will fail if the economic world keeps being driven by speculators who ignore the importance of added value. According to White, these speculators can easily provoke a crisis of unimaginable proportions, "a severe economic downturn, triggered by energy shocks, over-capacity in many extractive and manufacturing sectors, prolonged and widespread security crises, and failures of several global financial institutions and investment funds. A wave of multinational company downsizing and consolidation is underway, affecting thousands of suppliers and workers worldwide." Does this sound familiar in the wake of September 15, 2008?

To which De Regil Castilla adds, "…the fact is that all of these events are driven by the short term perceptions, expectations, speculations and manipulations of institutional investors. If this crisis occurs, it is precisely because governments would not rein in the market and would forswear once again and more profoundly their democratic responsibilities to procure the common good."

Against this position, the Liberal economic approach calls for little intervention by the state, leaving the market to flow according to its own laws. The dynamic discussion between these two approaches to socio-economic theory is not new. John Maynard Keynes and Milton Friedman initiated the discussion many years ago, both from the perspective of a capitalist society. Martin Wolf wrote in November, 2006 in the *Financial Times*: "The differences [between Keynes & Friedman] were, indeed, profound. But so was what they shared. More interesting, neither won and neither lost: today's policy orthodoxies are a synthesis of their two approaches…Keynes concluded from the Great Depression that the free market had failed; Friedman decided, instead, that the Federal Reserve had failed. Keynes trusted in discretion for sophisticated mandarins like himself; Friedman believed the only safe government was one bound by tight rules. Keynes thought that capitalism needed to be in fetters; Friedman thought it would behave if left alone."

Long term economic success, eventually, is built on moral foundations. An economy reflects the moral foundation of the community. The economic meltdown of 2008 is a clear reflection of the lack of moral principles in financial business in our world today. Usury and speculation are not new and their impact has been widely discussed by very prominent economists. Friedman believed that destabilizing speculation was impossible, that the market would correct itself and deliver long term democracy and prosperity. The reality has proved this argument wrong; the only way the world came out of the major six economic crises since 1980 has been through intervention by governments. Nowadays there is widespread awareness of the amount of monetary tools and resources that all governments are pouring into their economies to support ailing banks and major industries, like car manufacturers in the US.

If men don't have any self-restraint and don't feel guilt for their actions, an open system like the capitalist system is exposed to all kind of illnesses. The capitalist system is a good system. It can foster human development, wealth expansion, democratic governments, and equal opportunities, but it can be corrupted relatively easily by using its own instruments.

A mass of money of a certain size can artificially influence the value of goods, services, and companies up or down. Hedge funds can easily create a bubble by luring investors to buy an asset because of its perceived potential future value. At the same time, like a self-fulfilling prophecy, investors can bring a company down by short-selling and betting on that loss to happen.

You can win or lose, either way, betting on a gain or a loss. You just need to bet in the right direction. At this point in time I wonder if anybody really thinks that betting in the stock market is a terribly good idea for an individual. My hopes are gone. I bet on the crash and got my money out of the market before it happened. I think I was very lucky.

Forecasting in the short term today is almost impossible. Forecasting in the medium term is easier—the economic cycle theory does work and the tide goes up and down sooner or later. I wonder what the basic science behind this behavior is? Does the same thing happen on an individual basis? Do we experience the ups and downs? Is society's behavior a macro projection of individual behavior? If this is the case, it could be true for the good things, too; and men could model a society's behavior on the good moral values of its members and achieve a predictable outcome.

The main point of this book is that Corporate Social Responsibility is an incomplete approach to ensure long term business success. I also maintain that the CSR charter must follow the path toward integral human development if it is to become an important asset of every company. In this aspect we are far behind. Morality and social responsibility have not come together yet but that situation is changing, albeit slowly.

The fact that morality and social responsibility is coming together can be seen in the effort and size of the organizations that are now being created to deal with these problems. Most of them are based on the principles of diversity and inclusion. Different groups, that are coming from different angles, are getting together to establish a common ground of acceptable business social behavior.

An example of this is an organization called the Interfaith Center on Corporate Responsibility (ICCR). In this case, many different faith-based institutional investors have come together to work toward the implementation of a best-in-class corporate responsibility charter. For thirty-five years, the ICCR has been a leader of the corporate social responsibility movement. ICCR's membership is an association of 275 organizations including national denominations, religious communities, pension funds, foundations, hospital corporations, economic development funds, asset management companies, colleges, and unions. ICCR and its members press companies to be socially and environmentally responsible. Each year ICCR-member religious institutional investors sponsor over 200 shareholder resolutions on major social and environmental issues.

**ICCR core values, as presented in their Web site:**

- Faith-Based: "Faith guides and shapes our priorities for action."
- Justice: "We challenge ourselves and corporations to accountability for right relationships with all of creation."
- Integrity: "We are striving to be credible practitioners of the values we set forth."
- Inclusive: "We welcome diversity as we covenant to work together."

**And the priorities of ICCR members include:**

- eliminating sweatshops and corporate involvement in human rights abuses;
- reversing global warming;
- halting the proliferation of genetically modified foods until safety is proven;
- making capital available to all on an equal opportunity basis;
- working to make retailers of violent video games more accountable;
- making pharmaceuticals and healthcare safe, available and affordable to all;
- seeking more reasonable executive pay;

- seeking more accountable corporate governance structures; and

- stopping the use of depleted uranium weapons

It is encouraging that a large group of organizations, coming from such diverse backgrounds, can join their efforts to promote the implementation of socially responsible policies in corporations around the world. The ICCR has proposed hundreds of resolutions since 2005 and is scheduled to file 302 resolutions for 2008.

This group and others like it are actually helping to increase the awareness and sensitivity of our society towards real social issues. For the Christian faith and the Catholic Church, this has been the case since its inception two thousand years ago.

A complete set of principles, values, and behaviors provide a guide for all human interaction. CSR systems cannot regulate all aspects of in-the-job and out-of-the-job life of an individual as member of a company and it shouldn't. It is not the role of companies or governments to define people's behavior. They rely on the basic education and acceptable moral and ethical principles of individuals and communities. Many companies have unwritten rules that employees learn through unregulated ways that shape the "personality" of the company. What they call their "culture."

CSR systems will continue to evolve based on the demands of corporate stakeholders. It is unstoppable. It is evident now that environmental sustainability and the concern for climate change are in the forefront of many charters today. Sooner or later a human development agenda will get a big push coming from the increasing pressure from underdeveloped countries to share in the wealth of the rich world, and the need of affluent countries to develop markets in the underdeveloped world to sell their products and do business globally. The issue of immigration and diversity will also be part of the new wave of social issues that will drive changes in CSR charters. I am sure that, when these changes take place, the CSR model will mirror a more complete moral body.

The social doctrine of the Church already provides that comprehensive framework to enable all humans to reach their full potential, and for all human societies to enable it.

Regarding behavior, one fascinating experiment I once observed consisted of the following: a set of very simple machines, like small robots, obeying only two simple instructions that were based on the obstacles they encountered while moving randomly within a confined space. Objects of equal geometry but different color (black and white) were scattered through an enclosed area surrounded by a fence. If the machines moving straight ran into a black object they were supposed to pick it up, turn right and keep moving straight a certain distance and put the object back on the floor. If they ran into a white one, they were supposed to conduct another simple operation. The machines' starting location was random, the space where they could move was enclosed, and the objects were of the same geometry, two colors, and were scattered randomly.

After several minutes of random movements following those two simple operations on a complete chaotic environment, all the white pieces ended up grouped in one side of the area and all the black in the other side. Voila! It was like the act of an intelligent being.

This made me think so much! Could I explain this world and the human race based on this experiment? Could I explain at least economic and social behavior based on this experiment? Aren't we all a bunch of chaotic human-machines that can perform a limited number of operations and, in the end, what we all do as a society ends up looking, most of the time, like the action of an intelligent being?

What if we defined a set of simple social instructions like "Thou shall not kill" and simple economic instructions like "In the pursuit of gain do not misuse men as though they were things" to set up our simple economic system?

I came up with a list of possible simple instructions for my hypothetical dumb machine. I wanted to think that by executing all these instructions, men could develop a sound and intelligent economic system. My inner being drove me quickly to avoid any of the five economic cancers:

- Financial speculation and usury
- Corruption
- War
- The lack of respect for human life
- Lack of social conscience

Then I thought of the positive goals that I would like to promote into the system:

- Fair levels of profitability
- Reinvestment in the community
- Fair taxation
- Fair wages

I probably could have come up with hundreds more. It was getting too complicated. I stopped for a second and I realized my approach was wrong. It had to be much simpler. I believe in the simplicity of the Universe, the three primary colors, the seven basic musical notes, the four subatomic forces and

I suddenly started thinking of the very basic foundation of my moral system and I ended up realizing that there are only two basic and powerful simple instructions that would deliver my sound, socially responsible, sustainable economic and social system (Matthew 22:34-40):

"You shall love the Lord your God with all your heart, and with all your soul, and with all your mind."

*and*

"You shall love your neighbor as yourself."

This is not fundamentalism; this is rational thinking. It is all about recognizing where we are coming from, where we are going, who/what is the engine of our life, and that we would all like to be treated fair and square.

Should I participate actively in business activities that can make human beings suffer? Should I invest in companies that do not fit in my scheme of values? I must answer these questions, be honest with myself, and act accordingly.

# Chapter 4

## *"Blessed are they who hunger and thirst for righteousness, for they shall be satisfied."*

I found a parallelism between the development of CSR charters and the effort carried out by the Popes of the Catholic Church to develop a doctrine for all humans to deal with the social problems. During the research, it was very evident that what we today know as a Corporate Social Responsibility Charter is a subset of a more complete moral code. The Popes had already seen this analogy and, pressured by many Catholics who were "hungry and thirsty of righteousness," have since Leo XIII steadily defined a doctrine that was summarized and published in the *Compendium of the Social Doctrine of the Church* (Pontifical Council for Justice and Peace, 29 June, 2004).

It is shocking that the first *Compendium* wasn't published until the third millennium. In other religions, it has not been referenced yet. The encyclical *Rerum Novarum* by Leo XIII is recognized by all Christian denominations as the first powerful document that started to change the world of socio-economics.

Regarding other religious bodies: "Whether there exists as well a Protestant social doctrine comparable in extent and importance [to the Catholic one] or only a Protestant teaching on social ethics, is disputed even among Protestants themselves" (*Encyclopedia of Theology: A Concise Sacramentum Mundi* by Karl Rahner).

"Protestantism had largely accepted the compartmentalizing and secularizing of life which had been initiated by the Renaissance, and had been given special character in America by the notion of separation of church and state. The heritage of the frontier and revivalism made Protestants of the late nineteenth century individualistic to an unusual degree. At the very moment when a corporate approach to the emerging industrial problems was needed, Protestantism managed to lose its dynamism and ethical vitality, and in scholastic fashion thought of Christian truth as consisting of propositional statements that one comes by through an inward spiritual experience" (*The Social Gospel Part I*, Wake Forest University).

In the case of the Islamic faith, the Koran states that the real worth of a person's deeds can be judged only through *taqwa* (one's god-fearing devotion), and an individual's aim should be the ultimate benefit of humanity, not the immediate pleasures or ambitions of the self.

These principles of ethics and morals, combined with other beliefs and traditions, have motivated certain common behavior in all individuals belonging to the same community and following the same religious teachings. I could not find references of a written social doctrine for any religions other than the Catholic and the Orthodox Churches.

At the same time as the CSR movement has been evolving, we have to notice that since the first social encyclical was published in 1891 by Leo XIII, more than 1,000 documents have been released by the Popes and almost 50 percent of them deal, one way or another, with the "social question."

The most relevant ones are the following:

- *Rerum Novarum* (On the Condition of Workers). This encyclical of Leo XIII is considered by later Popes to be the foundational social justice teaching document of the modern era. Issued in 1891, it was a response to the changed conditions brought on by the Industrial Revolution.

- *Quadragesimo Anno* (On the Reconstruction of the Social Order). Issued in 1931, Pius XI reflects on the response of the Church and the world to *Rerum Novarum* forty years after Leo's document was disseminated.

- *Mater et Magistra* (Christianity and Social Progress). Issued by Pope John XXIII in 1961, this encyclical proposes methodologies for the application of Catholic teaching to concrete issues.

- *Pacem in Terris* (Peace on Earth). Issued by Pope John XXIII in 1963, this encyclical reflects on the rights of individuals and draws together two major strands of human rights thought: the Enlightenment ideals (of which the US Constitution and Bill of Rights are examples) and the older Catholic tradition of natural law rights.

- *Gaudium et Spes* (Pastoral Constitution on the Church in the Modern World). Promulgated in 1965 by the Second Vatican Council in union with Pope Paul VI, the Council continues to build on the foundation of "apostles and prophets" in applying church teachings to the modern world.

- *Inter Mirifica* (Decree on the Means of Social Communication). 1963, Vatican II

- *Lumen Gentium* (Dogmatic Constitution on the Church). 1964, Vatican II

- *Gravissimum Educationis* (Declaration on Christian Education). 1965, Vatican II

- *Populorum Progressio* (On the Development of Peoples). Encyclical issued in 1967 by Pope Paul VI. It considers the social and economic development of peoples and calls upon rich nations to assist the poor.

- *Octogesima Adveniens* (A Call to Action). Issued by Pope Paul VI in 1971, the Pope considers the Church in the city on the eightieth anniversary of *Rerum Novarum*.

- *Justitia in Mundo* (Justice in the World). Issued by the Synod of Bishops in 1971, this document is the source of the maxim "Work for social justice is a constituent element of preaching the Gospel."

- *Evangelii Nuntiandi* (Evangelization in the Modern World). This 1975 "Apostolic Exhortation" by Pope Paul VI links evangelism with social justice.

- *Laborem Exercens* (On Human Work). Issued in 1981 by Pope John Paul II, this encyclical reflects on a "theology of work" and "Christ the Worker."

- *Sollicitudo Rei Socialis* (On Social Concern). Issued by Pope John Paul II in 1987, this encyclical has an extensive discussion of solidarity and its role in Catholic teaching. In this document, John Paul II affirms the continuity of the Church's social doctrine in its links with the Gospel and its constant renewal due to changing conditions and events.

- *Centesimus Annus* (One Hundred Years). 1991 encyclical of Pope John Paul II that reflects on the hundred years of development of Catholic social justice teaching since *Rerum Novarum*. It contains important teachings on subsidiarity and the utility, and limits, of markets.

Such an extensive set of teachings was summarized in the document printed in 1984 called the *Compendium of the Social Doctrine of the Church*. This document, prepared by the Pontifical Council of Justice and Peace, is structured in the following chapters:

- An integral and solidary humanism (Introduction)
- God's plan of love for humanity
- The Church's mission and social doctrine
- The human person and human rights
- Principles of the Church's social doctrine
- The family, the vital cell of society
- Human work
- Economic life
- The political community
- Safeguarding the environment
- The promotion of peace
- Social doctrine and ecclesial action
- For a civilization of love (Conclusion)

The content of these documents forms a continuous reflection of:

- Man's behavior in regard to God, himself, family, community, society, and state

- The need for human development
- The role of the Catholic Church as teacher and advisor in social issues
- The need for social leadership by those who are able (individual and companies)
- A redefinition of the concept and meaning of work, economy, property, and common good

All these concepts overlap with the premises, actions, and consequences of CSR. The Church has not written yet a compendium on Corporate Social Responsibility, but she has certainly addressed all the components of a CSR charter and has developed a complete definition of the concept of social responsibility for all humans, not just for Catholics. "One would hope that also men and women without an explicit faith would be convinced that the obstacles to integral development are not only economic but rest on more profound attitudes which human beings can make into absolute values. Thus one would hope that all those who, to some degree or other, are responsible for ensuring a 'more human life' for their fellow human beings, whether or not they are inspired by a religious faith, will become fully aware of the urgent need to change the spiritual attitudes which define each individual's relationship with self, with neighbor, with even the remotest human communities, and with nature itself; and all of this in view of higher values such as the common good or, to quote the felicitous expression of the encyclical *Populorum Progressio*, the full development 'of the whole individual and of all people' " [SRS-38].

Why did Popes take upon themselves the need to write and teach about the "social question"? In each of these documents, the authors affirm their authority to understand and teach based on the following arguments:

- Because they are the chief guardians of the Catholic faith, as Leo XIII expresses, assuming full responsibility. "We approach the subject with confidence, and in the exercise of the rights which manifestly appertain to Us, for no practical solution of this question will be found apart from the intervention of religion and of the Church. It is We who are the chief guardian of religion and the chief dispenser of what pertains to the Church; and by keeping silence we would seem to neglect the duty incumbent on us" [RN-16].

- Forty years later, Pius XI states that people demanded at the end of the nineteenth century that the Church address the social question and the conditions of workers. "In such a sharp conflict of mind, therefore, while the question at issue was being argued this way and that, nor always with calmness, all eyes as often before turned to the Chair of Peter, to that sacred depository of all truth whence words of salvation pour forth to all the world. And to the feet of Christ's Vicar on earth were flocking in unaccustomed numbers, men well versed in social questions, employers, and workers themselves, begging him with one voice to point out, finally, the safe road to them" [QA-6].

- Pius XI goes further and proclaims that it resides in him, as Pope, the right and duty to pronounce with supreme authority upon social and economic matters and, in a conciliatory manner, expresses his desire to stay in the moral sphere and let men deal with the technical issues. "Certainly the Church was not given the commission to guide men to an only fleeting and perishable happiness but to that which is eternal. Indeed, the Church holds that it is unlawful for her to mix without cause in these temporal concerns; however, she [the Church] can in no wise renounce the duty God entrusted to her to interpose her authority, not of course in matters of technique for which she is neither suitably equipped nor endowed by office, but in all things that are connected with the moral law" [QA-40].

- John Paul II has a very optimistic message, stating that the Popes have not failed to throw fresh light by means of those messages upon new aspects of the social doctrine of the Church "to reaffirm the continuity of the social doctrine as well as its constant renewal. In effect, continuity and renewal are a proof of the perennial value of the teaching of the Church…typical of her teaching in the social sphere. On the one hand it is constant, for it remains identical in its fundamental inspiration, in its 'principles of reflection,' in its 'criteria of judgment,' in its basic 'directives for action,' and above all, in its vital link with the Gospel of the Lord. On the other hand, it is ever new, because it is subject to the necessary and opportune adaptations suggested by the changes in historical conditions and by the unceasing flow of the events which are the setting of the life of people and society" [SRS-3].

- John Paul II brings back the action of the Church to the dignity and rights of people: "It is not for the Church to analyze scientifically the consequences that these changes may have on human society. But the Church considers it her task always to call attention to the dignity and rights of those who work, to condemn situations in which that dignity and those rights are violated, and to help to guide the above-mentioned changes so as to ensure authentic progress by man and society" [LE-1].

The main issue is the acceptance by society of these arguments as valid. While reading the papal documents, it was quite noticeable that the Popes, in the beginning of their encyclicals, address the issue of authority. It was like a script that they were supposed to follow, like "I am talking about this because I have the moral authority, stature, and vision to do so."

There is naturally, an aura of prestige and charisma that comes with certain hierarchical positions. The papacy is probably one of the most charismatic. For Catholics, the Pope is the Vicar of Christ and his undisputable authority comes directly from the Holy Spirit, and lasts from his election to his death. Some aspects of their "magisterium" or teachings are considered Catholic dogma and can't be challenged; they are assumed to be revelations from God, forming the foundation of the entire body of faith. Some other teachings are not dogma and can be left open to analysis.

Because of this and intrinsic human freedom, there can be different interpretations of the non-dogmatic teachings of the Church. When it comes to social doctrine, the interpretations of people and cultures through history range from a communist Christ to a dictator God, with many other interpretations in between. It couldn't be any more confusing. As always, the truth might lie somewhere in the middle.

We will be able to position the social doctrine of the Church based on this statement by John Paul II wherein he affirms very clearly that the Church's social doctrine is not a "third way" between Liberal capitalism and Marxist collectivism, "…nor even a possible alternative to other solutions less radically opposed to one another: rather, it constitutes a category of its own. Nor is it an ideology, but rather the accurate formulation of the results of a careful reflection on the complex realities of human existence, in society and in the international order, in the light of faith and of the Church's tradition. Its main aim is to interpret these realities, determining their conformity with or divergence from the lines of the Gospel teaching on man and his vocation, a vocation which is at once earthly and transcendent; its aim is thus to guide Christian behavior. It therefore belongs to the field, not of ideology, but of theology and particularly of moral theology" [SRS- 41].

I know it is not very common to have a business book discuss morality. I sometimes find it very funny how well-known authors present theories based on human psychology but don't mention at all the spiritual aspect of any living being. It is a myopic vision. The intrinsic elements of motivation for workers, the motivation that is not connected to a prize, reward, or compensation, are founded on the very basic understanding of what the right thing to do might be, and how their responsibilities to the team and community are defined. This "right thing to do" is rooted in the moral code of the society where the worker lives and dies, and that morality is connected to the spiritual part of every person.

The intrinsic motivation of every person is therefore connected to the spirituality of that same person in connection with the group, either a team or a family or a community.

Spirituality and religion are also connected, one being the essence of the relationship with God and the second the specific manifestation of that relationship. Because of this, the Popes are entitled to spiritually lead humanity and offer a moral foundation for any human activity including social relationships, social responsibility, labor relations, and any other activity that involves the integral human person.

I always like to tell my teams that I will work hard to use their knowledge and skills. That everybody is extremely important to me, and that I want to have not only their brains, their wills and their hearts, I want to own their souls. The only way that the untapped possibilities of a team can blossom is by creating an environment where people feel and see that they are important in anything they say and anything they do.

I value the teachings of the Popes on social questions. I don't disagree on the "what" and I might have, in some cases, a different approach to the "how," but in essence I perceive their unconditional love for the human being as a creation of God, and I value their permanent contribution to guide all humanity onto the right track for human development.

# Chapter 5

## *"Blessed are the merciful, for they shall obtain mercy."*

**We get to the essence of this book.** We are going to walk together along a path surveying all social responsibility aspects of any given company, comparing what is now happening with the approach that the Catholic Church has advocated since 1891.

There is always a theological message from the Church to address human aspirations and needs. We can find these teachings in the *Compendium of the Social Doctrine of the Catholic Church* mentioned earlier.

My approach is less religious and more pragmatic, and takes into consideration the needs that executives consider when reflecting on these issues. I want to share a framework of thought that will enable company leaders to reflect before taking some decisions, and also highlight how important it is that they take a stance on these issues and act as social and economic leaders.

At the foundation of every economic system lies the concept of property. The concept of property, as such, is not an element of CSR charters but its interpretation has big consequences for different societies and companies. We could say that the way we understand property rights is at the core of our economic system, and directly influences the approach of companies to their social responsibility mission.

One of the most profound debates in the history of the industrialized world has centered on the concept of property. Who owns a company? Who owns its means of production? Who owns the labor and the products manufactured? How can we balance the concept of private property and the common good?

Property rights encompass the exclusive right of possessing, enjoying, and disposing of a thing. It is linked to the concept of ownership. Property, tangible or intangible, is a source of income or wealth and provides a right, title, or interest to one party to the exclusion of others.

The concept of property lies at the foundation of any social system. Company ownership confers a right to wealth and stability. The most stable way to engage employees with companies is based in the very simple concept of aligning the employees' self-interest with the interests of the company. This is the key equation for almost every enterprise. Think about this for just one second.

The most effective way to make this happen is to give the employees an opportunity to share in the wealth of the company and, ultimately, in its ownership. "The many proposals put forward by experts in Catholic social teaching and by the highest Magisterium of the Church take on special significance: proposals for joint ownership of the means of work, sharing by the workers in the management and/or profits of businesses, so-called shareholding by labor, etc." [LE-13].

"But it is unfortunate that on these new conditions of society a system has been constructed which considers profit as the key motive for economic progress, competition as the supreme law of economics, and private ownership of the means of production as an absolute right that has no limits and carries no corresponding social obligation" [PP-26].

History has seen in the twentieth century the rise and fall of social regimes based on Marxist ideas, socialist or communist.

At the same time, the world has seen the continuing development of a full capitalist system, a relatively new economic order that has not solved of all the world's problems either.

The Popes, since Leo XIII, have maintained a very clear doctrine on the concept of property. It could be summarized in the following propositions:

***The Church does not consider Marxism (communist or socialist) a solution to the "social question."***

*The first part of the Rerum Novarum is dedicated to socialism or any other type of collectivism. These are the six arguments against Marxism developed by Leo XIII in Rerum Novarum:*

1. First statement: Leo XIII understands human nature so well that he is able to foresee the effects of the application of Marxist theories on individuals, the family, societies, and the state in general. "They are, moreover, emphatically unjust, for they would rob the lawful possessor, distort the functions of the State, and create utter confusion in the community" [RN-4].

2. Second statement: "Man works to obtain property and to hold it as his very own." Leo later explains how the pursuit of private property drives human development. "Men have a right full and real to the disposal of their remunerations, just as he pleases. Socialism deprives of that liberty and with such of all hope and possibility of increasing his resources and of bettering his condition in life. It is surely undeniable that, when a man engages in remunerative labor, the impelling reason and motive of his work is to obtain property, and thereafter to hold it as his very own. If one man hires out to another his strength or skill, he does so for the purpose of receiving in return what is necessary for the satis-

faction of his needs; he therefore expressly intends to acquire a right full and real, not only to the remuneration, but also to the disposal of such remuneration, just as he pleases. Thus, if he lives sparingly, saves money, and, for greater security, invests his savings in land, the land, in such case, is only his wages under another form; and, consequently, a working man's little estate thus purchased should be as completely at his full disposal as are the wages he receives for his labor. But it is precisely in such power of disposal that ownership obtains, whether the property consist of land or chattels. Socialists, therefore, by endeavoring to transfer the possessions of individuals to the community at large, strike at the interests of every wage-earner, since they would deprive him of the liberty of disposing of his wages, and thereby of all hope and possibility of increasing his resources and of bettering his condition in life" [RN-5].

3. Third argument: "Every man has by nature the right to possess property as his own. This is one of the chief points of distinction between man and the animal creation" [RN-6].

4. Fourth argument: "Man precedes the State and possesses the right of providing substance for his body now and a later time. Planning and provision for the future is a man's responsibility" [RN-7]. This argument can clearly be defined as Liberal.

5. Fifth argument: "Those who deny these rights do not perceive that they are defrauding man of what his own labor has produced. For the soil which is tilled and cultivated with toil and skill utterly changes its condition; it was wild before, now it is fruitful; was barren, but now brings forth in abundance. That which has thus altered and improved the land becomes so truly part of itself as to be in great measure indistinguishable and

inseparable from it. Is it just that the fruit of a man's own sweat and labor should be possessed and enjoyed by any one else? As effects follow their cause, so is it just and right that the results of labor should belong to those who have bestowed their labor" [RN-10].

6. Sixth argument: The materialistic Marxism will create a society of slaves. "How intolerable and hateful slavery citizens would be subjected. Greed, invective, discord, sources of wealth will run dry, no interest, leveling down all conditions of degradation and misery. Socialism, community of goods, must be utterly rejected, since it only injures those whom it would seem meant to benefit, is directly contrary to the natural rights of mankind, and would introduce confusion and disorder into the commonweal. The first and most fundamental principle, therefore, if one would undertake to alleviate the condition of the masses, must be the inviolability of private property" [RN-15].

*All the Popes after Leo XIII have followed suit, and stated in all their social encyclicals their endorsement of Leo's original doctrine in support of "...the right of property against the tenets of the Socialists of his time by showing that its abolition would result, not to the advantage of the working class, but to their extreme harm" [QA-44].*

***Neither does the Church consider pure Liberalism an answer to the "social question":***

*"For the doctrine was preached that all accumulation of capital falls by an absolutely insuperable economic law to the rich, and that by the same law the workers are given over and bound to perpetual want, to the scantiest of livelihoods. It is true, indeed, that things have not always and everywhere corresponded with this sort of teaching of the so-called Manchesterian Liberals" [QA-54].*

*The doctrine of the Church "...differs from the programme of capitalism practiced by liberalism and by the political systems inspired by it. In the latter case, the difference consists in the way the right to ownership or property is understood. Christian tradition has never upheld this right as absolute and untouchable. On the contrary, it has always understood this right within the broader context of the right common to all to use the goods of the whole of creation: the right to private property is subordinated to the right to common use, to the fact that goods are meant for everyone" [LE-13].*

*Pius XI proclaims what I consider a cornerstone of the Church's social doctrine message: "Also the right ordering of economic life cannot be left to a free competition of forces. For from this source, as from a poisoned spring, have originated and spread all the errors of individualist economic teaching. Destroying through forgetfulness or ignorance the social and moral character of economic life, it held that economic life must be considered and treated as altogether free from and independent of public authority, because in the market, i.e., in the free struggle of competitors, it would have a principle of self direction which governs it much more perfectly than would the intervention of any created intellect. But free competition, while justified and certainly useful provided it is kept within certain limits, clearly cannot direct economic life" [QA-88]. This statement confronts Friedman's approach to economics.*

*Pius XI can't link a completely Liberal economic system to integral human development. He calls for free capitalism to be "kept within certain limits." And what are those limits? It is evident through the encyclicals that the limits are those that lead to integral and global human development. The right ordering of economic life cannot be left to a free competition of forces because "rich peoples enjoy rapid growth whereas the poor develop slowly. The imbalance is on the increase: some produce a surplus of foodstuffs, others cruelly lack them and see their exports made uncertain" [PP-8].*

***The Church understands property under God's plan for man and for creation. Property has a theological significance. It has to be connected to the idea of "common good."***

*"The right to private property is subordinated to the right to common use, to the fact that goods are meant for everyone" [LE-13].*

*The Popes maintain that there is a clear difference between the right to private property and the right to use: "At the same time it differs from the programme of capitalism practiced by liberalism and by the political systems inspired by it. In the latter case, the difference consists in the way the right to ownership or property is understood. Christian tradition has never upheld this right as absolute and untouchable. On the contrary, it has always understood this right within the broader context of the right common to all to use the goods of the whole of creation: the right to private property is subordinated to the right to common use, to the fact that goods are meant for everyone" [LE-13].*

*If there should arise a conflict "between acquired private rights and primary community exigencies," it is the responsibility of public authorities "to look for a solution, with the active participation of individuals and social groups" [PP-23].*

*Pius XI reinforces the connection of the right to use with the spiritual laws. He affirms that there is no legal action to force owners to use property the right way but under the spiritual laws. "A principle established by Leo XIII: The right of property is distinct from its use. That justice called commutative commands sacred respect for the division of possessions and forbids invasion of others' rights through the exceeding of the limits of one's own property; but the duty of owners to use their property only in a right way does not come under this type of justice, but under other virtues, obligations of which 'cannot be enforced by legal action.' Therefore, they are in error who assert that ownership and its right use are limited by the same boundaries; and it is much farther still from the truth to hold that a right to property is destroyed or lost by reason of abuse or non-use" [QA-47].*

*The Church's teaching has always expressed the strong and deep conviction that man's work concerns not only the economy but also, and especially, personal values. "The economic system itself and the production process benefit precisely when these personal values are fully respected. In the teachings of Saint Thomas Aquinas, this is the principal reason in favour of private ownership of the means of production" [LE-15].*

*The Church's social doctrine is not a "third way" between Liberal capitalism and Marxist collectivism, "...nor even a possible alternative to other solutions less radically opposed to one another: rather, it constitutes a category of its own. Nor is it an ideology, but rather the accurate formulation of the results of a careful reflection on the complex realities of human existence, in society and in the international order, in the light of faith and of the Church's tradition. Its main aim is to interpret these realities, determining their conformity with or divergence from the lines of the Gospel teaching on man and his vocation, a vocation which is at once earthly and transcendent; its aim is thus to guide Christian behavior. It therefore belongs to the field, not of ideology, but of theology and particularly of moral theology" [SRS-41].*

***The Church understands the role of industrialization and technology and considers such progress very positive for the welfare of men.***

As John Paul II states, "The very process of 'subduing the earth,' that is to say, work, is marked in the course of history, and especially in recent centuries, by an immense development of technological means. This is an advantageous and positive phenomenon, on condition that the objective dimension of work does not gain the upper hand over the subjective dimension, depriving man of his dignity and inalienable rights or reducing them" [LE-10].

John Paul II is immersed in a technological world that is viewed by him with *gaudium et spes*, happiness and hope. He considers the issue of human work as the central issue of the "social question" and looks at technology as a good thing because it is also a result of human work. All means of production, from the most primitive to the ultramodern, have been gradually developed by man, using his experience and intellect. In this way there have appeared not only the simplest instruments for cultivating the earth but also, through substantial progress in science and technology, more modern and complex ones: machines, factories, laboratories, and computers. "Thus, everything that is at the service of work, everything that in the present state of technology constitutes its ever more highly-perfected 'instrument,' is the result of work" [LE-12].

At the same time, John Paul II makes sure we don't assign to technology too much responsibility for human development. "The mere accumulation of goods and services, even for the benefit of the majority, is not enough for the realization of human happiness. Nor, in consequence, does the availability of the many real benefits provided in recent times by science and technology, including the computer sciences, bring freedom from every form of slavery. On the contrary, the experience of recent years shows that unless all the considerable body of resources and potential at man's disposal is guided by a moral understanding and by an orientation towards the true good of the human race, it easily turns against man to oppress him" [SRS-28].

The permanent balancing act of linking every premise, argument, or inference to man as the center of God's creation can be found in all the documents I researched: everything is good or bad depending on its interaction with the history of man's salvation and God's plan for men.

***The Church states that the problems generated within any social or economic order are created by men because of what Pius XI calls the "economic sins":***

> *The unquenchable thirst for riches;*
>
> *The use of means, fair or foul, to protect their wealth against changes of fortune;*
>
> *Buying and selling of goods with the only aim of making quick profits with the least expenditure of work (speculation);*
>
> *Raising or lowering prices rapidly according to their own caprice and greed, nullifying the wisest forecast of producers;*
>
> *The lack of conscience or accountability of directors (and industry leaders);*
>
> *Hiding behind corporate name, the directors of business companies, forgetful of their trust, betray the rights of those whose savings they have undertaken to administer;*
>
> *Crafty men, unconcerned about any honest usefulness of their work, do not scruple to stimulate the baser human desires and exploit them for their own profit.*

Recently the Church has published a list of social sins. The sins are obviously not new, but the list is. It has been grouped this way to help everybody understand and recognize their own responsibility in certain critical areas of human life. The new list is the following:

1. Genetic modification
2. Carrying out experiments on humans
3. Polluting the environment
4. Causing social injustice
5. Causing poverty
6. Becoming obscenely wealthy
7. Taking drugs

In this line of thought, Paul VI affirms: "But if it is true that a type of capitalism has been the source of excessive suffering, injustices, and fratricidal conflicts whose effects still persist, it would also be wrong to attribute to industrialization itself evils that belong to the woeful system which accompanied it. On the contrary, one must recognize in all justice the irreplaceable contribution made by the organization of labor and of industry to what development has accomplished" [PP-26].

***The Church's vision is based on the Christian notion of social justice. The Popes understand that the struggle for human development is legitimate. "Following the lines laid down by the Encyclical Rerum Novarum and many later documents of the Church's Magisterium, it must be frankly recognized that the reaction against the system of injustice and harm that cried to heaven for vengeance and that weighed heavily upon workers in that period of rapid industrialization was justified from the point of view of social morality. This state of affairs was favored by the liberal socio-***

***political system, which, in accordance with its 'economistic' premises, strengthened and safeguarded economic initiative by the possessors of capital alone, but did not pay sufficient attention to the rights of the workers, on the grounds that human work is solely an instrument of production, and that capital is the basis, efficient factor and purpose of production" [LE-8].***

To quote Saint Ambrose: "You are not making a gift of your possessions to the poor person. You are handing over to him what is his. For what has been given in common for the use of all, you have arrogated to yourself. The world is given to all, and not only to the rich." That is, private property does not constitute for anyone an absolute and unconditioned right. No one is justified in keeping for his exclusive use what he does not need, when others lack necessities. In a word, "according to the traditional doctrine as found in the Fathers of the Church and the great theologians, the right to property must never be exercised to the detriment of the common good."

Leo XIII defines "laws of social justice" in a way that forms the entire social doctrine of the Church:

> *First law of social justice: Men have the right to own land, the means of production, and companies. That will create a bridge between the wealthy and the working people. "If working people can be encouraged to look forward to obtaining a share in the land, the consequence will be that the gulf between vast wealth and sheer poverty will be bridged over, and the respective classes will be brought nearer to one another" [RN-47].*

> *Second law of social justice: Men always work harder and more readily when they work on that which belongs to them. Bring people to the ownership of the company or to share in its economic success. "A further consequence will result in the great abundance of the fruits of the earth.*

*Men always work harder and more readily when they work on that which belongs to them; nay, they learn to love the very soil that yields in response to the labor of their hands, not only food to eat, but an abundance of good things for themselves and those that are dear to them. That such a spirit of willing labor would add to the produce of the earth and to the wealth of the community is self-evident" [RN-47].*

*Third law of social justice: Give men the opportunity to find prosperity in their own land and eradicate the need to migrate if not desired. "Men would cling to the country in which they were born, for no one would exchange his country for a foreign land if his own afforded him the means of living a decent and happy life" [RN-47].*

*Fourth law of social justice: Men should not be deprived of more than is fair through taxation. "Those three important benefits, however, can be reckoned on only provided that a man's means be not drained and exhausted by excessive taxation. The right to possess private property is derived from nature, not from man; and the State has the right to control its use in the interests of the public good alone, but by no means to absorb it altogether. The State would therefore be unjust and cruel if under the name of taxation it were to deprive the private owner of more than is fair" [RN-47].*

*Fifth law of social justice: Men have the right to have a system that takes care of those much in need. "In the last place, employers and workmen may of themselves effect much, in the matter We are treating, by means of such associations and organizations as afford opportune aid to those who are in distress, and which draw the two classes more closely together. Among these may be enumerated societies for mutual help; various benevolent foundations established by private persons to provide for the workman, and for his widow or his orphans, in case of sudden calamity, in sickness, and in the event of death; and institutions for the welfare of boys and girls, young people, and those more advanced in years" [RN-48].*

*Sixth law of social justice: The right to association. "Men establish relations in common with one another in the setting up of a commonwealth." And later on: "Private societies, then, although they exist within the body politic, and are severally part of the commonwealth, cannot nevertheless be absolutely, and as such, prohibited by public authority. For, to enter into a 'society' of this kind is the natural right of man; and the State has for its office to protect natural rights, not to destroy them; and, if it forbid its citizens to form associations, it contradicts the very principle of its own existence, for both they and it exist in virtue of the like principle, namely, the natural tendency of man to dwell in society" [RN-51].*

*Seventh law of social justice: The right to have men's religious duties and morality as the most essential component of any social betterment. "We may lay it down as a general and lasting law that working men's associations should be so organized and governed as to furnish the best and most suitable means for attaining what is aimed at, that is to say, for helping each individual member to better his condition to the utmost in body, soul, and property. It is clear that they must pay special and chief attention to the duties of religion and morality, and that social betterment should have this chiefly in view; otherwise they would lose wholly their special character, and end by becoming little better than those societies which take no account whatever of religion. What advantage can it be to a working man to obtain by means of a society material well-being, if he endangers his soul for lack of spiritual food? 'What doth it profit a man, if he gains the whole world and suffers the loss of his soul?' [RN-57].*

Pius XI elaborates on the criticism of unsound economic systems that don't strive for the realization of the common good. "To each, therefore, must be given his own share of goods, and the distribution of created goods, which, as every discerning person knows, is laboring today under the gravest evils due to the huge disparity between the few exceedingly rich and the unnumbered property-less, must be effectively called back to and brought into conformity with the norms of the common good, that is, social justice" [QA-58].

***The Church always looks to implement the Truth. There is no relativism in the moral foundation of the Church. When dealing with the concept of property, its logical argument is based on the premise that private property is natural and in accordance with God's law, and the affirmation that if the use of that private property is a right, then the social system that develops will be sound. On the other hand, if the use of the property is wrong and damages the common good, then the social system is not sound and must be changed.***

In this last case, exceptions to the rule are allowed, as Paul VI states: "If certain landed estates impede the general prosperity because they are extensive, unused or poorly used, or because they bring hardship to peoples or are detrimental to the interests of the country, the common good sometimes demands their expropriation" [PP-24].

Certainly this is one of the most controversial statements in all the documents I have studied regarding the social doctrine of the Church. Paul VI doesn't say "demands its collectivization" since he doesn't believe that collective property under the rule of the state is a sound social policy. But he does mention the word "expropriation," which means taking away the property from someone who legally owns it. Who has the right to expropriate? Who determines how "good" is the "common good"? I doubt that, at any given time, there will be an objective body that can determine that an expropriation is fair enough. In most cases of expropriation, conflict will happen. Should governments expropriate from individuals in Western economies in order to provide free land or company ownership to individuals who have nothing? Is taxation a form of expropriation?

As the world moves away from collectivist systems, the Popes suggest a balance to pure capitalism by introducing in the discussion some room for alternative systems that have some elements of collectivism:

> *John Paul II understands, but doesn't promote, the need to collectivize property in some cases but at the same time expresses again his support for controlled implementation of socialized property under the condition that the worker continues feeling that he works for himself. "While we accept that for certain, well-founded reasons, exceptions can be made to the principle of private ownership [the right to private property]—in our own time we even see that the system of 'socialized ownership' has been introduced—nevertheless the personalist argument still holds good both on the level of principles and on the practical level. If it is to be rational and fruitful, any socialization of the means of production must take this argument into consideration. Every effort must be made to ensure that in this kind of system also the human person can preserve his awareness of working 'for himself.' If this is not done, incalculable damage is inevitably done throughout the economic process, not only economic damage but first and foremost damage to man" [LE-15].*

> *"In the Church's teaching, ownership has never been understood in a way that could constitute grounds for social conflict in labor...., property is acquired first of all through work in order that it may serve work. This [issue] concerns in a special way ownership of the means of production. Isolating these means as a separate property in order to set it up in the form of 'capital' in opposition to 'labor'—*

*and even to practice exploitation of labor—is contrary to the very nature of these means and their possession. They cannot be possessed against labor, they cannot even be possessed for possession's sake, because the only legitimate title to their possession—whether in the form of private ownership or in the form of public or collective ownership—is that they should serve labor, and thus, by serving labor, that they should make possible the achievement of the first principle of this order, namely, the universal destination of goods and the right to common use of them. From this point of view, therefore, in consideration of human labor and of common access to the goods meant for man, one cannot exclude the socialization, in suitable conditions, of certain means of production" [LE-13].*

*The Church does not have technical revolutions to offer for the problem of underdevelopment as such, as Pope Paul VI already affirmed in his encyclical. "For the Church does not propose economic and political systems or programs, nor does she show preference for one or the other, provided that human dignity is properly respected and promoted, and provided she herself is allowed the room she needs to exercise her ministry in the world" [SRS-41].*

Some of these statements can certainly be seen as radical and in contradiction with the traditional doctrine of the Church. We have to remember that the entire system of teachings of the Church is based on premises that are nonnegotiable, mainly the need for every single economic system to have a positive effect on man and be aligned with God's precepts. The Church asks of everyone self-sacrifice for the common good and hopes that eventually this will happen and no drastic measures will have to be applied. The Church also recognizes that evil is part of man, too, and that our selfishness will impede us from giving generously and helping others share our success and our company's success. In those cases, the Church has tough words and does not compromise with evil.

The best solutions for all social issues are found through the understanding of how we connect with the global plan for humankind. The solutions come from our soul, not from our minds.

# Chapter 6

## *"Blessed are the pure of heart, for they shall see God."*

### Morality

Corporate Social Responsibility opened the window of fresh, pure, air into business management. Ethical behavior, sustainable development, climate change and energy conservation activities, increase of employee participation, diversity—are all concepts developed under the umbrella of Corporate Social Responsibility.

LJ Thompson, in his article in the *Journal of Leadership and Organizational Studies* (Vol. 11), proposes a definition for morality "…to include a spiritual dimension without privileging religion: A framework of vision, values, practice, and performance that defines and shapes character, especially in the conditions of danger, risk, and uncertainty."

The same author affirms, "Effective leaders are able to engage with others in building by example and constructive effort, an environment within which individuals and groups are free and encouraged to discern and actualize the right and the good in fulfillment of shared goals, values and purpose.…Leaders of corporations, communities, and nations hesitate to speak confidently in a single, authoritative 'corporate' voice; the public voices of corporate enterprises are expected to project the values and interests of the diverse stakeholders who constitute them."

Adel Safty, in his article "Moral Leadership. Beyond Management and Governance," is more emphatic in his view of the responsibility of company leaders: "Leadership, on the other hand is, or at least ought to be, normatively apprehended as a set of values with connotations evocative of the higher achievements of the human spirit. Leadership, therefore, is irrevocably tied to morality. Measured by its results, leadership in whatever field should be the vision-driven achievements of those people who are able to transform their environment, morally elevate their followers, and chart new paths of progress and human development. As a concept, leadership should mean a set of values dedicated to promoting human development for the common good of people in a democratic environment, both at the national and international levels."

All Popes call for social responsibility and social leadership. Paul VI calls "particularly to those whose education, position and opportunities afford them wide scope for action." There is a need for social leaders to emerge from the economic and educational world who could drive the improvement of our community forward. Paul VI says, "We want to be clearly understood: the present situation must be faced with courage and the injustices linked with it must be fought against and overcome. Development demands bold transformations, innovations that go deep. Urgent reforms should be undertaken without delay. It is for each one to take his share in them with generosity, particularly those whose education, position, and opportunities afford them wide scope for action" [PP-32].

Paul VI shows an incredible respect for individual freedom and responsibility to decide how to collaborate with God in His creation. The Pope is absolutely convinced that men will do the right thing acting on "their own conscience enlightened by God's law authentically interpreted, and sustained by confidence in

Him." There will be no mistake, no evil, and no wrong decision. Indirectly, the Pope is affirming that the liberty and leadership of man has to be founded on very solid moral rock. "In all this they must follow the demands of their own conscience enlightened by God's law authentically interpreted, and sustained by confidence in Him" [PP-37].

The concept of Corporate Moral Leadership is being shaped nowadays. John E. Kelly, from the Department of Philosophy at Canisius College (Buffalo, NY), writes: "One of the crucial intellectual and social challenges facing corporation leaders is to foster a new way of thinking about business and society which recognizes the multinational corporation as a key player in society's responsibility to support and maintain fairness in the global reorganization of markets. In order to establish a sound global social economy, we are in need of the organizing and directing principles of solidarity and subsidiarity."

No different from what the Church has been advocating for long time.

As executives, the main goal that we may pursue in our professional life is to use our talents, our experience, and our time to enable our employees, their families, the employees of our customers and suppliers and their families, and in general all people and communities directly or indirectly impacted by our decisions and actions, to develop themselves as human beings, by providing a fair job with fair compensation, education, and training, and connecting their success to the success of the company we work for.

We have to assume moral and social leadership and we have to make sure that our opportunities are used to create a positive impact on the common good.

In this time, the social doctrine of the Church underscores the importance of options for business leaders to set the right foundation for their programs. The business leader is "endowed with intelligence and freedom; he is responsible for his fulfillment as he is for his salvation" [PP-15].

At the heart of Corporate Social Responsibility, and of any religion, is the man, not an economic man but an integral man. As Paul VI says, "Development cannot be limited to mere economic growth. In order to be authentic, it must be complete: integral, that is, it has to promote the good of every man and of the whole man. As an eminent specialist has very rightly and emphatically declared: We do not believe in separating the economic from the human, or development from the civilizations in which it exists. What we hold important is man, each man and each group of men, and we even include the whole of humanity" [PP-14].

## The balanced approach to profitability

For a business to be successful, income must be greater than expenses. The company must find the optimum size with respect to its market and prevailing economic conditions to efficiently service its customers. Business success requires the right strategies and investments in people, process, and technology. For many companies it is not a problem to understand and execute capital investments in equipment—they get it, they buy a machine that will produce a product they can see. Even fewer companies can understand and execute capital investments in processes (e.g., ISO 9001, ISO 14000, Lean tools, 6 sigma tools) based on the cost reduction opportunities and the improvement of operational effectiveness they can deliver. But the fewest companies understand and support the need to invest in their people. Machines will not make things happen. People do.

How much investment—resources that eventually come out of the assets of the company—are executives willing to spend on people? How many companies really do understand that a short term approach to people can provoke a medium or long term strategic problem that will be extremely difficult to overcome? Companies cannot be successful if they don't balance and synchronize their actions and investments on people, process, and technology.

The Popes offer several suggestions on how to bring employees to share in the success of the companies: "We consider it more advisable, however, in the present condition of human society that, so far as is possible, the work-contract be somewhat modified by a partnership-contract, as is already being done in various ways and with no small advantage to workers and owners. Workers and other employees thus become sharers in ownership or management or participate in some fashion in the profits received" [QA-65].

In a way, Leo XIII asked companies to invest in their employees by providing enough time and resources for their own development:

"The following duties bind the wealthy owner and the employer: not to look upon their work people as their bondsmen, but to respect in every man his dignity as a person ennobled by Christian character. They are reminded that, according to natural reason and Christian philosophy, working for gain is creditable, not shameful, to a man, since it enables him to earn an honorable livelihood; but to misuse men as though they were things in the pursuit of gain, or to value them solely for their physical powers—that is truly shameful and inhuman. Again justice demands that, in dealing with the working man, religion and the good of his soul must be kept in mind. Hence, the employer is bound to see that the worker has time for his religious duties; that he be not exposed to corrupting influences and dangerous occasions; and that he be not led away to neglect his home and family, or to squander his earnings. Furthermore, the employer must never tax his work people beyond their strength, or employ them in work unsuited to their sex and age. His great and principal duty is to give every one what is just. Doubtless, before deciding whether wages are fair, many things have to be considered; but wealthy owners and all masters of labor should be mindful of this—that to exercise pressure upon the indigent and the destitute for the sake of gain, and to gather one's profit out of the need of another, is condemned by all laws, human and divine. To defraud any one of wages that are his due is a great crime which cries to the avenging anger of Heaven. 'Behold, the hire of the laborers...which by fraud has been kept back by you, crieth; and the cry of them hath entered into the ears of the Lord of Sabbath.' Lastly, the rich must religiously refrain from cutting down the workmen's earnings, whether by force, by fraud, or by usurious dealing; and with all the greater reason because the laboring man is, as a rule, weak and unprotected, and because his slender means should in proportion to their scantiness be accounted sacred" [RN-20].

Also, some of the "economic sins" I mentioned before deal with the issue of profits [QA-132]:

- Unquenchable thirst for riches;

- Buying and selling of goods with the only aim of making quick profits with the least expenditure of work;

- The lack of conscience or accountability of directors;

- Crafty men, unconcerned about any honest usefulness of their work, do not scruple to stimulate the baser human desires and exploit them for their own profit.

German ex-Chancellor Gerhard Schroeder summarized the key issue of balanced profitability in a speech delivered to factory workers: "It has been revealed that egotism practiced at the top under the catchphrase 'shareholder value' is worth less in macroeconomic terms, but also as far as the companies themselves are concerned, than a system based on a fair balance between the interests of the employees and the employers."

A traditional organization (for-profit or not-for-profit) is characterized by:

- top-down decision-making,
- [with] restricted participation of employees,
- concentration of power at the top of the organization, and
- limited information about the organization available to employees;
- capital investors and employees usually being different people;
- maximization of economic benefits primarily to reward capital investors;
- objectives of investors, managers, and workers often inconsistent with each other; and
- voluntary economic contribution to the community.

A Christian-based organization will be based on the following principles:

- the dignity of the human person, which is the foundation of all the other principles and content of the Church's social doctrine;
- social justice: the common good—to which every aspect of social life must be related if it is to attain its fullest meaning—stems from the dignity, unity and equality of all people;

- economic justice: subsidiarity by which all societies of a superior order must adopt attitudes of help ("subsidium")—therefore of support, promotion, development—with respect to lower-order societies;

- solidarity, which emphasizes the intrinsically social nature of the human person, the equality of all in dignity and rights, and the common path of individuals and peoples towards an ever more-committed unity.

Christian organizations will recognize management leadership but will push hard for full employee involvement with full access to company information. The interests of investors, managers, and employees would be aligned, and the ultimate objective would be to make the company an agent of human development at all levels (personal and communities and social groups) in the global market. Ownership of the company will be open and accessible to all employees, whose main target is to pursue holiness for the organization as an entity. Probably this last statement raised some eyebrows.

In my professional experience, the companies that I have seen growing successfully have the following two things in common:

- They knew how to align their employees' self-interest with the interest of the company.

- They knew how to maximize the utilization of the knowledge and skills of their work force.

I understand training to be a tool and a facilitator. Every bit of training must have its own ROI (return on investment). It has to be clearly defined what is going to change after the training is completed. What process or procedure, role or responsibility will be different and what are the expectations? Training is probably one of the most second-guessed investments in people at any company.

I have been thinking for some time on a way to capture employee contribution to the success of a company. I have developed a model in my mind but I haven't used it yet. It is based on the following matrix:

| | **Compensated** | **Not Compensated** |
|---|---|---|
| **Mandatory participation** | | |
| **Voluntary participation** | | |

My hypothesis is that the companies that log more hours in voluntary non-compensated time are more successful. I would like to define an Employee Involvement Index that would take these four quadrants into consideration. The theory will be completed if I can relate a company's performance to the Employee Involvement Index. One day I will try to complete it.

The reality is that if companies don't have a way to consistently deliver their mission via employee willingness, sooner or later they disappear.

Customers, suppliers, community, government, and employees have an expectation of results from any company. Can companies in the long term deliver on these promises if they don't take care of their people, and look very narrowly to short term profits? It is, again, the world of speculators looking for quick money that selfishly expose people to an uncertain future. I admire those companies that allocate a percentage of their income toward innovation, and that moderate their profitability by reinvesting in the company, its people, products and equipment, the community at large, and the global village they operate in.

## Ethical consumerism

A liberalism based on corporations that "care" seems to be the new social and economical model, with "care" defined as a self-imposed code of ethics based on the natural law that is accepted by customers, employees, and shareholders.

Citizens as consumers are defining what is acceptable and shaping a new global social order. Conscious citizens—assuming their responsibility in the management of global natural resources, the integration of people of many diverse backgrounds, the role of education, a concern for safety and health, respect for individual beliefs and religious rituals, and many more areas—are taking a stand today and are telling the companies that control the world that they demand a guarantee of sustainability and viability for future generations.

Ours is a "Civilization of 'consumption' or 'consumerism,' which involves so much 'throwing-away' and 'waste.' An object already owned but now superseded by something better is discarded, with no thought of its possible lasting value in itself, nor of some other human being who is poorer. All of us experience firsthand the sad effects of this blind submission to pure consumerism: in the first place a crass materialism, and at the same time a radical dissatisfaction, because one quickly learns—unless one is shielded from the flood of publicity and the ceaseless and tempting offers of products—that the more one possesses the more one wants, while deeper aspirations remain unsatisfied and perhaps even stifled" [SRS-28].

"Thus, part of the teaching and most ancient practice of the Church is her conviction that she is obliged by her vocation—she herself, her ministers and each of her members—to relieve the misery of the suffering, both far and near, not only out of her 'abundance' but also out of her 'necessities.' Faced by cases of need, one cannot ignore them in favor of superfluous church ornaments and costly furnishings for divine worship; on the contrary it could be obligatory to sell these goods in order to provide food, drink, clothing and shelter for those who lack these things" [SRS-31].

Did you read the same thing I did? Is John Paul II saying that the Church should sell "all superfluous church ornaments and costly furnishings for divine worship…in order to provide food, drink, clothing and shelter for those who lack these things"? How great he was! Has anybody ever reflected on these teachings?

Did my local parish ever think of giving the $3 million they raised to fix a beautiful church and the rectory to the poor who live perhaps less than 50 miles from us? We are all condemned; my only hope is that God is so merciful that He will make exceptions and let some go through to His glory.

## Fiscal responsibility

Leo XIII defines the path for prosperity: "Now a State chiefly prospers and thrives through moral rule, well-regulated family life, respect for religion and justice, the moderation and fair imposing of public taxes, the progress of the arts and of trade, the abundant yield of the land—through everything, in fact, which makes the citizens better and happier" [RN-32].

And Paul VI states very clearly that this can be achieved only through the contribution to society by those who have more, through proper taxation. He usually speaks with tougher words: "Government officials, it is your concern to mobilize your peoples to form a more effective world solidarity, and above all to make them accept the necessary taxes on their luxuries and their wasteful expenditures, in order to bring about development and to save the peace" [PP-84].

Paul VI wants the government to set the goals, provide resources, but avoid controlling community/society initiatives.

He encourages private initiative and what he calls "intermediate bodies" to exercise their fundamental rights.

"Hence programs are necessary in order to encourage, stimulate, coordinate, supplement and integrate the activity of individuals and of intermediary bodies. It pertains to the public authorities to choose, even to lay down the objectives to be pursued, the ends to be achieved, and the means for attaining these, and it is for them to stimulate all the forces engaged in this common activity. But let them take care to associate private initiative and intermediary bodies with this work. They will thus avoid the danger of complete collectivization or of arbitrary planning, which, by denying liberty, would prevent the exercise of the fundamental rights of the human person" [PP-33].

Fair taxation, always looking for the appropriate balance, is the final destination. As Leo said in the nineteenth century, "These three important benefits, however, can be reckoned on only provided that a man's means be not drained and exhausted by excessive taxation. The right to possess private property is derived from nature, not from man; and the State has the right to control its use in the interests of the public good alone, but by no means to absorb it altogether. The State would therefore be unjust and cruel if under the name of taxation it were to deprive the private owner of more than is fair" [RN-47].

We all know of people who play the game of shifting income from some countries to others. Some do it through permanent residency schemes, some through artificial transfer costs between divisions of the same holding. For all those, this is what Paul VI has to say: "Consequently it is unacceptable that citizens with abundant incomes from the resources and activity of their country should transfer a considerable part of this income abroad purely for their own advantage, without care for the manifest wrong they inflict on their country by doing this" [PP-24].

Then I thought over what I do and how I approach things and I couldn't find an answer to the following questions: "But neither all this nor the private and public funds that have been invested, nor the gifts and loans that have been made, can suffice. It is not just a matter of eliminating hunger, nor even of reducing poverty. The struggle against destitution, though urgent and necessary, is not enough. *It is a question, rather, of building a world where every man, no matter what his race, religion or nationality, can live a fully human life*, freed from servitude imposed on him by other men or by natural forces over which he has not sufficient control; a world where freedom is not an empty word and where the poor man Lazarus can sit down at the same table with the rich man. This demands great generosity, much sacrifice and unceasing effort on the part of the rich man. Let each one examine his conscience, a conscience that conveys a new message for our times. Is he prepared to support out of his own pocket works and undertakings organized in favor of the most destitute? Is he ready to pay higher taxes so that the public authorities can intensify their efforts in favor of development? Is he ready to pay a higher price for imported goods so that the producer may be more justly rewarded? Or to leave his country, if necessary and if he is young, in order to assist in this development of the young nations?" [PP-47].

Sometimes I would like to think I didn't read this, but once you do, it is almost impossible to ignore. How can I, as a business executive, address all these challenging issues in my professional life, never mind my personal life? Am I willing to push my company to pay, out of pocket, for works in favor of the most destitute? I can certainly answer Yes to this one, but how much is good enough? How much outreach is good enough? Is there a limit to solidarity?

The next challenge is also somewhat simple: Am I, or my company, willing to pay more taxes to intensify development activities? I haven't yet met someone who would request higher taxes on his own money. I have heard politicians asking for that when talking about other people's money. Do we really trust public officials?

Do we really think that the government can execute development activities better than individuals and organizations? In my case I have to answer No. Could governments accomplish with the same amount of money what the Catholic Church, and many other NGOs, can do for human development on a global basis? I bet it would cost ten times more. Giving and outreaching doesn't need to come in the way of higher taxation but in a net increase of all contributions, taxes and no taxes, to human development. We should develop a Human Development Index to measure the contributions of individuals and companies to human development. I am sure this will come up soon in the evolution of Corporate Social Responsibility.

I already said earlier that taxation should shift from productive activities and job creation to unproductive and speculative activities. This is the main move that I would like governments to undertake.

The third question is very tough: Are companies willing to pay more for imported products to favor human development in poor countries? If we consider raw material purchases as 50 percent of product cost, that means that for every 10 percent more that a company pays for its goods, the gross margin shrinks by 5 percent. Paying more than the price a company can get in the global market, following fair standard practices, seems to go against all basic economic principles. Sooner or later, unless every company paid more, the companies that do so will lose their own market share and cease generating income for those poor countries. Fewer companies will offer the product, enabling them to drive down the prices even further, with an end result of more poverty and misery. I think that we shouldn't try to subsidize poor countries through the pricing of goods; I would propose that it be done through mandatory reinvesting of free cash flow generated by the company in those countries where it operates globally, based on the amount of trade that occurs between the rich company and its suppliers in those low-cost countries. It ties in to the fair levels of profitability that we discussed earlier.

# Chapter 7

## *"Blessed are the peacemakers, for they shall be called children of God."*

**There is a moral reason for work.** "Man must work, both because the Creator has commanded it and because of his own humanity, which requires work in order to be maintained and developed. Man must work out of regard for others, especially his own family, but also for the society he belongs to, the country of which he is a child, and the whole human family of which he is a member, since he is the heir to the work of generations and at the same time a sharer in building the future of those who will come after him in the succession of history. All this constitutes the moral obligation of work" [LE-16].

The main concerns for the Popes are, in the first place, that every man has access to a job to support his own development, and that of his family and community; the second is that the job is compensated fairly and there are rules that take into consideration all the physical and spiritual needs of the worker.

On the fairness of wages, all the encyclicals advance the topic front and center very consistently: "The basis for determining the value of human work is not primarily the kind of work being done but the fact that the one who is doing it is a person" [LE-6].

- "Wages, as we are told, are regulated by free consent, and therefore the employer, when he pays what was agreed upon, has done his part and seemingly is not called upon to do anything beyond. The only way, it is said, in which injustice might occur would be if the master refused to pay the whole of the wages, or if the workman should not complete the work undertaken; in such cases the public authority should intervene, to see that each obtains his due, but not under any other circumstances" [RN-43].

- "Before deciding whether wages are fair, many things have to be considered; but wealthy owners and all masters of labor should be mindful of this—that to exercise pressure upon the indigent and the destitute for the sake of gain, and to gather one's profit out of the need of another, is condemned by all laws, human and divine. To defraud any one of wages that are his due is a great crime which cries to the avenging anger of Heaven" [RN-20].

- "Let the working man and the employer make free agreements, and in particular let them agree freely as to the wages; nevertheless, there underlies a dictate of natural justice more imperious and ancient than any bargain between man and man, namely, that wages ought not to be insufficient to support a frugal and well behaved wage-earner" [RN-45].

- "If a workman's wages be sufficient to enable him comfortably to support himself, his wife, and his children, he will find it easy, if he be a sensible man, to practice thrift, and he will not fail, by cutting down expenses, to put by some little savings and thus secure a modest source of income" [RN-46].

- "In determining the amount of the wage, the condition of a business and of the one carrying it on must also be taken into account; for it would be unjust to demand excessive wages which a business cannot stand without its ruin and consequent calamity to the workers. If, however, a business makes too little money, because of lack of energy or lack of initiative or because of indifference to technical and economic progress, that must not be regarded a just reason for reducing the compensation of the workers. But if the business in question is not making enough money to pay the workers an equitable wage because it is being crushed by unjust burdens or forced to sell its product at less than a just price, those who are thus the cause of the injury are guilty of grave wrong, for they deprive workers of their just wage and force them under the pinch of necessity to accept a wage less than fair" [QA-72].

- "The amount of the pay must be adjusted to the public economic good" [QA-74]. Pius XI links the lowering and the raising of wages beyond "proper limits" with the unemployment rate in many countries. "For everyone knows that, an excessive lowering of wages, or their increase beyond due measure, causes unemployment."

- "A right proportion among wages and salaries" [QA-75]. The relationship of wages among all the layers of the organization must be considered. How much more should a CEO receive compared to an average worker? We could cite cases of inflated stock value that led to incredible executive compensation that proved to be pure manipulation. Should speculation be rewarded? Where is the responsibility of company directors to guarantee the long term performance of their companies and fair compensation?

- "The relationship between the employer (first and foremost the direct employer) and the worker is resolved on the basis of the wage, that is through just remuneration for work done" [LE-19].

- "Wages, that is to say remuneration for work, are still a practical means whereby the vast majority of people can have access to those goods which are intended for common use: both the goods of nature and manufactured goods. Both kinds of goods become accessible to the worker through the wage which he receives as remuneration for his work. Hence, in every case, a just wage is the concrete means of verifying the justice of the whole socioeconomic system and, in any case, of checking that it is functioning justly. It is not the only means of checking, but it is a particularly important one and, in a sense, the key means" [LE-19].

But we said it is not only the wages but all the physical and spiritual conditions that need to be addressed: "A new branch of law, wholly unknown to the earlier time, has arisen from this continuous and unwearied labor to protect vigorously the sacred rights of the workers that flow from their dignity as men and as Christians. These laws undertake the protection of life, health, strength, family, homes, workshops, wages and labor hazards, in fine, everything which pertains to the condition of wage workers, with special concern for women and children" [QA-28].

If there is any doubt of what the Catholic Church thinks of health insurance, paid vacation and holidays, pension and retirement, working conditions, physical health, and moral integrity, John Paul II explains them very clearly in *Laborem Exercens*:

"Besides wages, various social benefits intended to ensure the life and health of workers and their families play a part here. The expenses involved in health care, especially in the case of accidents at work, demand that medical assistance should be easily available for workers, and that as far as possible it should be cheap or even free of charge. Another sector regarding benefits is the sector associated with the right to rest. In the first place this involves a regular weekly rest comprising at least Sunday, and also a longer period of rest, namely the holiday or vacation taken once a year or possibly in several shorter periods during the year. A third sector concerns the right to a pension and to insurance for old age and in case of accidents at work. Within the sphere of these principal rights, there develops a whole system of particular rights which, together with remuneration for work, determine the correct relationship between worker and employer. Among these rights there should never be overlooked the right to a working environment and to manufacturing processes which are not harmful to the workers' physical health or to their moral integrity" [LE-19].

Living in a country that has 45 million people without health coverage, these words of hope from the Pope are very meaningful and rewarding. It appeals to my safety, health, and environmental conscience. They give meaning to all my efforts to achieve best-in-class status as a company that safely produces a quality product at a competitive cost in many countries.

Finally, John Paul II has words of encouragement to those who support some type of social support system: "The obligation to provide unemployment benefits, that is to say, the duty to make suitable grants indispensable for the subsistence of unemployed workers and their families, is a duty springing from the fundamental principle of the moral order in this sphere, namely the principle of the common use of goods or, to put it in another and still simpler way, the right to life and subsistence" [LE-18].

Of course, when you read these things you start remembering those people in your career who knew how to play the system and profited from unemployment benefits, medical leave, bereavement and attendance policies, and the like, and you start thinking that all these welfare policies are a drain on the sustainable economic well-being of any society. I am not going to dispute that. I think of those people myself. And then I read John Paul's words and I see him imploring me to consider the fact that some people's abuse of the system is not reason enough to neglect all those who really need it. Governments should deal more harshly with those who manipulate social programs. It should be considered a crime against humanity and carry severe penalties.

## Work environment, respect, and dignity

We already addressed working conditions earlier. I want to make a point now regarding people with physical and mental challenges in our society. The Popes, in their gracious understanding of human beings, do not leave any room for ambiguity when telling the world that disabled people have the right to belong to the working world according to their particular capacities.

"Careful attention must be devoted to the physical and psychological working conditions of disabled people—as for all workers—to their just remuneration, to the possibility of their promotion, and to the elimination of various obstacles. Without hiding the fact that this is a complex and difficult task, it is to be hoped that a correct concept of labor in the subjective sense will produce a situation which will make it possible for disabled people to feel that they are not cut off from the working world or dependent upon society, but that they are full-scale subjects of work, useful, respected for their human dignity and called to contribute to the progress and welfare of their families and of the community according to their particular capacities" [LE-22].

I have been connected to industries that employ disabled people and I have been witness to their incredible work. I have been moved by the way the educational system in Massachusetts integrates handicapped kids like my own daughter, and provides what is required to help them develop their full human potential. I praise their work; it will never be sufficiently rewarded. This is a serious problem for society and I thank John Paul II for his words. I hope society can be generous enough to help all disabled individuals achieve their maximum level of human dignity and development.

"The disabled person is one of us and participates fully in the same humanity that we possess. It would be radically unworthy of man, and a denial of our common humanity, to admit to the life of the community, and thus admit to work, only those who are fully functional. To do so would be to practice a serious form of discrimination, that of the strong and healthy against the weak and sick. Work in the objective sense should be subordinated, in this circumstance too, to the dignity of man, to the subject of work and not to economic advantage" [LE-22].

For all workers in any organization, I like the way Dr. J. Robert Ouimet, in his article "Reconciliation of Profits and Human Wellbeing: Is It Too Late?", defines the list of values that any organization should support to enable full employee integration and participation:

"**Solidarity**—Employees who gain better understanding of their colleagues will also develop a greater sense of compassion for their well being, and belonging in the workplace. In this context, work can be a legitimate place to grow intellectually, socially, and even spiritually.

**Dignity**—Employees must be treated as ends in themselves, not as means to an end. This axiom invariably encourages managers to base their management techniques and decisions on the primacy of human dignity, and not essentially on mercantile considerations.

**Respect**—The hallmark of good communications is the ability to listen to others, understand their concerns, appreciate their ideas, and encourage their opinion; in short, demonstrate respect for others, their wants and needs. This enables people the opportunity to express themselves, be more productive, happier, and more personally fulfilled.

**Faith and hope**—It is essential, for many more people than we think in the workplace, to have faith and hope in a greater power.

It does not need to be characterized as a religious entity, but it must instill some spiritual aspiration, such as serving the physical and social well-being of employees. Such sensibility will insure economic decisions, will take into consideration the primacy of human dignity, and emphasize that work does exist for people and not people for work. This working environment, in a climate of solidarity, dignity, respect and faith, enables individuals to see a greater meaning to work and life.

**Caring and appreciation—**Shareholders and management must find the courage to do what is good and right and to communicate to others their authentic caring and appreciation for their contributions, sacrifice and dedication to the company, other personnel, customers, family, and community. Such gestures have a profound impact on the psychic and physical well-being of every worker in the organization

”

## Diversity

For many companies I know, diversity is understood as the strategy to avoid costly lawsuits, and is implemented through literal translations of some advertisements into languages spoken by minorities and the achievement of an acceptable level of minority representation at all levels of the organization. They don't understand that diversity is about integrating cultures and engaging people regardless of their values. "Among still other obstacles which are opposed to the formation of a world which is more just and which is better organized toward a universal solidarity, We wish to speak of nationalism and racism" [PP-62].

Again, all Popes address this issue front and center in a cohesive set of teachings that condemn any discrimination on the basis of national origin, sex, age, religion, or cultural discrepancies.

"However, the picture just given would be incomplete if one failed to add to the 'economic and social indices' of underdevelopment other indices which are equally negative and indeed even more disturbing, beginning with the cultural level. These are illiteracy, the difficulty or impossibility of obtaining higher education, the inability to share in the building of one's own nation, the various forms of exploitation and of economic, social, political and even religious oppression of the individual and his or her rights, discrimination of every type, especially the exceptionally odious form based on difference of race. If some of these scourges are noted with regret in areas of the more developed North, they are undoubtedly more frequent, more lasting and more difficult to root out in the developing and less advanced countries" [SRS-15].

I personally thank the Popes for their unambiguous opposition to nationalism. There are people in this world who will always use the difference between humans as an excuse to discriminate against individuals and create oppositional groups. They will foment conflict, with the only final result being poverty and misery. "Freed of all nationalistic pride and of every appearance of racism, experts should learn how to work in close collaboration with all....Mutual understanding will be established which will enrich both cultures" [PP-72].

"Racism...is still an obstacle to collaboration among disadvantaged nations and a cause of division and hatred within countries whenever individuals and families see the inviolable rights of the human person held in scorn, as they themselves are unjustly subjected to a regime of discrimination because of their race or their color" [PP-63].

The case for diversity is based on the notion that we gain by being different. Based on the theory of evolution, only diverse populations can survive in the long term. Diversity makes us stronger and more resilient; it makes sense from a technical and biological standpoint.

From a business point of view, it makes a lot of sense, too. Teams exist because individuals are extremely limited. We each possess only a limited amount of knowledge and skills in a limited amount of categories, and in a finite time span and finite geographical location. To face some problems we need to work with other people who expand our capabilities.

In my professional life I always follow certain rules to create teams. I believe that some people are very good identifying problems, some others finding out the root causes, some other proposing solutions, and some others implementing them. I always try to have those skills in any team I form. To achieve my goal, I certainly need to select team members who can contribute some of these talents. If I get the right mix of knowledge and skills, the likelihood of success is very high. They team members don't need to be the brightest, but they have to complement one another on those skills.

I also look for a range of temperaments, for people who, for example, have entrepreneurial, producer, administrative, or teaching attributes. These various traits are necessary in order to form a high-performance team. Some of them will be leaders, some facilitators, some enablers, some followers. In the end, it is the cohesive team performance that delivers results. "There naturally exist among mankind manifold differences of the most important kind; people differ in capacity, skill, health, strength; and unequal fortune is a necessary result of unequal condition. Such inequality is far from being disadvantageous either to individuals or to the community. Social and public life can only be maintained by means of various kinds of capacity for business and the playing of many parts; and each man, as a rule, chooses the part which suits his own peculiar domestic condition" [RN-17].

## Education

The Popes look at education from four different angles:

*As a cause of social development or underdevelopment.*

The delay in cultural advances, education, and literacy is the main cause for social underdevelopment. "However, the picture just given would be incomplete if one failed to add to the 'economic and social indices' of underdevelopment other indices which are equally negative and indeed even more disturbing, beginning with the cultural level. These are illiteracy, the difficulty or impossibility of obtaining higher education, the inability to share in the building of one's own nation, the various forms of exploitation and of economic, social, political and even religious oppression of the individual and his or her rights, discrimination of every type, especially the exceptionally odious form based on difference of race. If some of these scourges are noted with regret in areas of the more developed North, they are undoubtedly more frequent, more lasting and more difficult to root out in the developing and less advanced countries" [SRS-15].

*As a enabler of freedom.*

The Popes repeat forever their conviction that there is no freedom without truth and that there is no truth and development without the proper education. "Freedom from misery, the greater assurance of finding subsistence, health and fixed employment; an increased share of responsibility without oppression of any kind and in security from situations that do violence to their dignity as men; better education" [PP-6].

*As an enabler of sustainable societies.*

It is critical that we use the resources at hand to rescue underdeveloped people from the miseries of hunger, and it is as important to rescue them from the misery of lack of basic education. The only way societies can be sustainable is through the progress of their people achieved through education from childhood. "It can even be affirmed that economic growth depends in the very first place upon social progress: thus basic education is the primary object of any plan of development. Indeed hunger for education is no less debasing than hunger for food: an illiterate is a person with an undernourished mind. To be able to read and write, to acquire a professional formation, means to recover confidence in oneself and to discover that one can progress along with the others" [PP-35].

- Education plays a significant role in the formation of a structured, successful society and it facilitates many opportunities for labor. "The organization of human life in accordance with the many possibilities of labor should be matched by a suitable system of instruction and education, aimed first of all at developing mature human beings, but also aimed at preparing people specifically for assuming to good advantage an appropriate place in the vast and socially differentiated world of work" [LE-18].

*As an enabler for men to fulfill God's plans.*

How can all men fulfill God's plans if they are deprived of the basic means to fulfill his vocation? "In the design of God, every man is called upon to develop and fulfill himself, for every life is a vocation. At birth, everyone is granted, in germ, a set of aptitudes and qualities for him to bring to fruition. Their coming to maturity, which will be the result of education received from the environment and personal efforts, will allow each man to direct himself toward the destiny intended for him by his Creator" [PP-15].

- Children especially must be given the chance to get "outside of the hole" of misery. "Too early an experience of life's hard toil blights the young promise of a child's faculties, and renders any true education impossible" [RN-42].

- "Work and industriousness also influence the whole process of education in the family, for the very reason that everyone 'becomes a human being' through, among other things, work, and becoming a human being is precisely the main purpose of the whole process of education" [LE-10].

- "Two aspects of work in a sense come into play here: the one making family life and its upkeep possible, and the other making possible the achievement of the purposes of the family, especially education" [LE -10].

John Paul II is very pragmatic again when he points out that not all education is effective: "An ever increasing number of people with degrees or diplomas in the fields of their cultural preparation are accompanied by a drop in demand for their labor. This unemployment of intellectuals occurs or increases when the education available is not oriented towards the types of employment or service required by the true needs of society, or when there is less demand for work which requires education, at least professional education, than for manual labor, or when it is less well paid" [LE-8].

One of the aspects of my professional career so far that makes me proudest is the impact on real people of my training programs and communication. I like to classify training in three different categories:

**Survival training. Basic training including among others:**

- Second language

- Basic literacy (reading/writing)

- Basic primary degrees

**Technical training (oriented to trade specialists). Examples are:**

- Machine operators
- Plumbers, electricians, etc.
- ISO standards
- Lean tools
- Transactional Enterprise Resources Planning systems

**Advanced training like:**

- Advanced analysis and optimization
- Six Sigma tools for business excellence
- Robotics, PLC, and automation
- Systems integration

When I received a present from one of the classes of English as a Second Language that I sponsored, I felt a real sense of accomplishment. They presented me with a card in which all of them expressed (in English) their experiences as members of the class. From that day forward, they had the opportunity to qualify for jobs that required basic literacy in English. Some of them went on to enroll in a class to become a basic machine operator, and landed a job that had been out their reach for many years. From there, they continued their education, they aspired to more, and they achieved higher levels of responsibility. For many years they hadn't been able to move out of non-skilled jobs and suddenly, within three years, they were able to assume very high levels of responsibility because of their higher levels of competency.

Training increases the morale of organizations. But training for the sake of training can be useless, as John Paul II reminded us before. The training has to be SMART, like the goals for any organization:

- Specific
- Measurable
- Attainable
- Realistic
- Timely

The impact of training has to be planned before the action happens. Two important questions have to be answered:

- What is going to change in the process, procedure, role or responsibilities of the person receiving the training?
- How is the organization going to sustain the changes and eventually improve and optimize over time?

## Employee participation

The most difficult challenge that companies face is how to engage their own people. Only engaged employees can engage customers. One employee could kill a company.

When I think of this issue, I try to phrase the challenge the following way: How can I align employees' self interest with the company's interest?

There are many theories of motivation that model people's behavior. Of course, I like the various theories of X, Y and Z that were developed in the last part of the last century, but I also like to reflect on motivation from another angle. Some behavioral experts talk about intrinsic and extrinsic (or internal and external, if that is easier) sources of motivation. I do believe that the willingness of a person who says "I can and I will" is the final reward for any motivational strategy.

What can bring a person to say that? Some people say that they have to have "some skin in the game," that a system of sharing the success or the defeat should be in place. In my experience I have seen these extrinsic systems work (like gain-sharing) and not work (like profit-sharing). But in any case, I have seen teams perform at an incredible rate, without any extrinsic motivation, when they felt they had:

- Challenge
- Control
- Cooperation
- Recognition
- Fun
- Trust

"Men always work harder and more readily when they work on that which belongs to them; nay, they learn to love the very soil that yields in response to the labor of their hands, not only food to eat, but an abundance of good things for themselves and those that are dear to them" [RN-47].

I would also like to add the following "musts" if you want to achieve high levels of employee participation and release untapped levels of productivity:

- Employees have to be part of the strategic cycle of the companies. They have to contribute.

- Companies must have a sound Breakthrough Deployment tool to link the goals for the organization with the individual objectives of its employees.

- All employees must have a way to link their daily performance in all the values with the final objectives of the team.

- Managers have to be facilitators. For that matter, the most important aspect is the communication that generates "common action."

- Employees and managers, together, have to review their performance and generate continuous improvement initiatives.

- Celebrate and have fun in the process.

- Be fair and consistent with your decisions as a manager and lead by example.

The Popes also shed some light on how they interpret the solution to the employee engagement challenge. "We consider it more advisable, however, in the present condition of human society that, so far as is possible, the work-contract be somewhat modified by a partnership-contract, as is already being done in various ways and with no small advantage to workers and owners. Workers and other employees thus become sharers in ownership or management or participate in some fashion in the profits received" [QA-5].

CSR does not deal with the issue of employee motivation. It does assume that people make things happen and mostly addresses the role of men as part of the community, including the working community. The motivation that is intrinsic to CSR is based on the belief that people will share common values that transcend the temporality of their employment, even their lives; there is a common understanding and acceptance of what is the right thing to do and people will find intrinsic reasons to do the right things.

I find this notion difficult to implement if there is no common goal or understanding of what the "common greater good" is, and I am not sure this can be found outside of the spiritual being. Intrinsic motivation, the willingness of an individual to say "I can and I will" is founded on the spiritual rock. You can't buy it with money.

# Chapter 8

## *"Blessed are they who are persecuted for the sake of righteousness, for theirs is the kingdom of heaven."*

### Human Development—Globalization

The "social question" has evolved from a class issue (East-West conflict) to a world issue (North-South) and seemingly affects the entire globe. Economic globalization is acting as an equalizer in different aspects of human development. We can cite, among others, these four important aspects affecting business:

- It is enabling cultural exchanges that are in some cases increasing—and in others, decreasing—the understanding of different societies and the acceptance of new products.

- It is helping to create a middle class in developing countries in Asia and Latin America that can afford a new, higher standard of living.

- It is giving all societies the opportunity to access media to receive information essential to their own development and to make choices in the global business arena.

- It is allowing high-cost countries to redefine their manufacturing and supply chain footprint by relocating production to low-cost countries. With this move, some companies are certainly addressing their product offering to a global market, while some others, unfortunately, are just using it to generate speculative short term gains.

"Today the principal fact that we must all recognize is that the social question has become world-wide" [PP-3]. "At the same time social conflicts have taken on world dimensions" [PP-9].

"While in the past the 'class' question was especially highlighted as the centre of this issue, in more recent times it is the 'world' question that is emphasized. Thus, not only the sphere of class is taken into consideration but also the world sphere of inequality and injustice, and as a consequence, not only the class dimension but also the world dimension of the tasks involved in the path towards the achievement of justice in the modern world" [LE-2].

There are very critical issues in today's world that have to be analyzed on a global scale:

- Impact of the transfer of manufacturing jobs from rich economies to poor economies

- The interconnectedness of financial markets

- The interconnectedness of commodity markets

- The issue of migration

- Fundamentalism and the war on terror

- Dependence on oil and the issue of the end of fossil fuels

- Climate change and its impact on global food availability
- The issue of human development

Regarding the outsourcing of manufacturing jobs from rich economies to poor economies, John Paul II, recognizing the severe impact on people, shares a reflection that for some might be shocking: “These new conditions and demands will require a reordering and adjustment of the structures of the modern economy and of the distribution of work. Unfortunately, for millions of skilled workers these changes may perhaps mean unemployment, at least for a time, or the need for retraining. They will very probably involve a reduction or a less rapid increase in material well-being for the more developed countries. But they can also bring relief and hope to the millions who today live in conditions of shameful and unworthy poverty” [LE-1].

It is clear that John Paul II asks for a sacrifice that can bring progress to those poor countries that don’t have any other way of getting out of misery.

“There can be no progress towards the complete development of man without the simultaneous development of all humanity in the spirit of solidarity” [PP-43].

At the same time, the Pope asks governments to be sensitive to these issues and provide the proper training and opportunities for people to move to other jobs. The Church wants to be a guide for all those people affected so that there is authentic progress for man and society. Global solidarity comes at a price that many societies are not willing to assume.

“It is not for the Church to analyze scientifically the consequences that these changes may have on human society. But the Church considers it her task always to call attention to the dignity and rights of those who work, to condemn situations in which that dignity and those rights are violated, and to help to guide the above-mentioned changes so as to ensure authentic progress by man and society" [LE-1].

John Paul II expresses in his *Laborem Exercens* one of the most devastating criticisms of our current global economic order. Rich companies, trying to maximize their profits by squeezing margins of low-cost producers, end up impacting the conditions of the poorest workers on this world. And the rich world looks the other way when these issues are brought to light.

"...it can easily become an occasion for various forms of exploitation or injustice...For instance the highly industrialized countries, and even more the businesses that direct on a large scale the means of industrial production (the companies referred to as multinational or transnational), fix the highest possible prices for their products, while trying at the same time to fix the lowest possible prices for raw materials or semi-manufactured goods. This is one of the causes of an ever increasing disproportion between national incomes. The gap between most of the richest countries and the poorest ones is not diminishing or being stabilized but is increasing more and more, to the detriment, obviously, of the poor countries. Evidently this must have an effect on local labor policy and on the worker's situation in the economically disadvantaged societies. Finding himself in a system thus conditioned, the direct employer fixes working conditions below the objective requirements of the workers, especially if he himself wishes to obtain the highest possible profits from the business which he runs (or from the businesses which he runs, in the case of a situation of 'socialized' ownership of the means of production)" [LE-17].

Paul VI has a vision of a perfect and solidary world. When reading these statements I remember Hume's *homo homini lupus* (the man is a wolf to man)—a beast, with no mercy or compassion for anybody, ready to destroy the weak and continue his way through life, taking no prisoners. On the other end of the spectrum I find my Christian faith that gives a new goal, a new frontier and hope to people, and affirms that, regardless of all the circumstances that don't let us behave fraternally, there is a humane way forward that is within our reach. It is our willingness to individually say Yes to this call that will transform the world.

"Between civilizations, as between persons, sincere dialogue indeed creates brotherhood. The work of development will draw nations together in the attainment of goals pursued with a common effort if all, from governments and their representatives to the last expert, are inspired by brotherly love and moved by the sincere desire to build a civilization founded on world solidarity. A dialogue based on man, and not on commodities or technical skills, will then begin. It will be fruitful if it brings to the peoples who benefit from it the means of self betterment and spiritual growth, if the technicians act as educators, and if the instruction imparted is characterized by so lofty a spiritual and moral tone that it guarantees not merely economic, but human development. When aid programs have terminated, the relationships thus established will endure. Who does not see of what importance they will be for the peace of the world?" [PP-73].

Paul VI continues his recommendations on how to conduct business globally. In the following statement He clearly asks a very simple question: Why do you follow inhumane principles of individualism in other countries when you would not dare doing it in yours?

"Our second recommendation is for those whose business calls them to countries recently opened to industrialization: industrialists, merchants, leaders or representatives of larger enterprises. It happens that they are not lacking in social sensitivity in their own country; *why then do they return to the inhuman principles of individualism when they operate in less developed countries?* Their advantaged situation should on the contrary move them to become the initiators of social progress and of human advancement in the area where their business calls them. Their very sense of organization should suggest to them the means for *making intelligent use of the labor of the indigenous population, of forming qualified workers, of training engineers and staffs, of giving scope to their initiative, of introducing them progressively into higher positions, thus preparing them to share, in the near future, in the responsibilities of management.* At least let justice always rule the relations between superiors and their subordinates. Let standard contracts with reciprocal obligations govern these relationships. Finally, let no one, whatever his status, be subjected unjustly to the arbitrariness of others" [PP-70].

This is precisely the reason why the outsourcing of American production to Mexico in the '90s failed, and the outsourcing to Asia succeeded. In the Mexican case, the companies were managed remotely by Americans and no ownership or responsibility was bestowed on the Mexican teams. The few companies that enjoyed real success implemented a team concept to involve the employees in the production lines and employ local management to run the companies.

Also important for many companies is the issue of global sustainability. Some companies take credit for a reduction of greenhouse gases in their domestic operations, even those with manufacturing activities in developing countries. This is absolutely phenomenal if that reduction is calculated considering their entire value chain. If the reduction is achieved by the outsourcing of their product to countries that will not follow any rules for environmental sustainability, then the net effect might be negative and their sustainability record is a lie. The question that all companies should ask themselves is: What is the net effect of changing the global manufacturing and supply chain footprint for my company regarding the sustainability promise made to society?

For the Church, it is immoral to inflict misery and pain on people by manufacturing our products in less than desirable working conditions. "On the path toward the desired conversion, toward the overcoming of the moral obstacles to development, it is already possible to point to the positive and moral value of the growing awareness of interdependence among individuals and nations. The fact that men and women in various parts of the world feel personally affected by the injustices and violations of human rights committed in distant countries, countries which perhaps they will never visit, is a further sign of a reality transformed into awareness, thus acquiring a moral connotation" [SRS-38].

Solidarity and respect for the sovereignty of weaker nations. "Surmounting every type of imperialism and determination to preserve their own hegemony, the stronger and richer nations must have a sense of moral responsibility toward the other nations, so that a real international system may be established which will rest on the foundation of the equality of all peoples and on the necessary respect for their legitimate differences. The economically weaker countries, or those still at subsistence level, must be enabled, with the assistance of other peoples and of the international community, to make a contribution of their own to the common good with their treasures of humanity and culture, which otherwise would be lost forever" [SRS-39].

A positive aspect is that we certainly have, since the Declaration of Human Rights, a frame of reference to act morally regarding the impact of our businesses in the global village: "At this level one must acknowledge the influence exercised by the Declaration of Human Rights, promulgated some forty years ago by the United Nations Organization. Its very existence and gradual acceptance by the international community are signs of a growing awareness. The same is to be said, still in the field of human rights, of other juridical instruments issued by the United Nations Organization or other international organizations" [SRS-26].

## Human Development—Individual

John XXIII's teaching is important and its application urgent: "Today the peoples in hunger are making a dramatic appeal to the peoples blessed with abundance" [PP-3].

History shows that human progress always generates a residual amount of evil; there are always groups that are left behind—groups that don't have access to the common wealth of the community, that have no opportunity to access the level of education that will take them out of the "hole."

We are called to act fast, but with equilibrium. Reforms have to be implemented at a speed that can be tolerated by communities. There cannot be a setback in human values.

"We must make haste: too many are suffering, and the distance is growing that separates the progress of some and the stagnation, not to say the regression, of others. Yet the work required should advance smoothly if there is not to be the risk of losing indispensable equilibrium. A hasty agrarian reform can fail. Industrialization if introduced suddenly can displace structures still necessary, and produce hardships in society which would be a setback in terms of human values" [PP-29].

The task is so huge that it can only happen through effort and planning. "The present situation calls for concerted planning. A planned program is, of course, better and more effective than occasional aid left to individual goodwill. It presupposes, as We said above, careful study, the selection of ends and the choice of means, as well as a reorganization of efforts to meet the needs of the present and the demands of the foreseeable future. More important, a concerted plan has advantages that go beyond the field of economic growth and social progress; for in addition it gives significance and value to the work undertaken. While shaping the world it sets a higher value on man" [PP-50].

The cancers of society will hinder all these efforts. They are so difficult to eradicate that sometimes everyone feels hopeless. I refer to:

- Financial speculation

- Corruption
- War
- Lack of respect for human life
- Lack of social conscience

Any of these can kill action toward peace and social justice.

I thought about wealth, and Leo XIII provides me with the answer I can live with: "Those who are engaged in producing goods, therefore, are not forbidden to increase their fortune in a just and lawful manner; for it is only fair that he who renders service to the community and makes it richer should also, through the increased wealth of the community, be made richer himself according to his position, provided that all these things be sought with due respect for the laws of God and without impairing the rights of others and that they be employed in accordance with faith and right reason. If these principles are observed by everyone, everywhere, and always, not only the production and acquisition of goods but also the use of wealth, which now is seen to be so often contrary to right order, will be brought back soon within the bounds of equity and just distribution" [RN-133].

In the end it is not what you are given; it is about how you react and use what you have for the benefit of the entire human race.

## Human Development—Family

This is my favorite subject. This is my most immediate community, where I practice all my talents, my faith, and my spirituality twenty-four/seven.

- "A family, no less than a State, is, as We have said, a true society, governed by an authority peculiar to itself" [RN-13].

- "A family is simultaneously a community made possible by work and the first school of work, within the home, for every person" [LE-10].

- "Hence we have the family, the 'society' of a man's house—a society very small, one must admit, but nonetheless a true society, and one older than any State. Consequently, it has rights and duties peculiar to itself which are quite independent of the State" [RN-12].

The family, as a true society, enjoys rights at least equal to society in general, if not more so, because it preceded society. "The family has at least equal rights with the State in the choice and pursuit of the things needful to its preservation and its just liberty. We say, 'at least equal rights'; for, inasmuch as the domestic household is antecedent, as well in idea as in fact, to the gathering of men into a community, the family must necessarily have rights and duties which are prior to those of the community, and founded more immediately in nature" [RN-13].

If there is a very common theme of human motivation, it is the appeal to promote the advancement of those we consider our family. It is a responsibility and, most of the times, a joy and a privilege. "Through work man must earn his daily bread and contribute to the continual advance of science and technology and, above all, to elevating unceasingly the cultural and moral level of the society within which he lives in community with those who belong to the same family" [LE-1].

The social question has its foundation also in man as member of a family: "Work constitutes a foundation for the formation of family life…work is a condition for making it possible to found a family, since the family requires the means of subsistence which man normally gains through work" [LE-10].

For the Church, the rights of a family are probably the most important rights. The Church sees the family as a local "church" where the promises of God are fulfilled, and where the correspondence of its members with the Holy Family can be understood more easily. A family that compares well with the Holy Family is probably the number one goal for the Church.

"The rights here spoken of, belonging to each individual man, are seen in much stronger light when considered in relation to man's social and domestic obligations. In choosing a state of life, it is indisputable that all are at full liberty to follow the counsel of Jesus Christ as to observing virginity, or to bind themselves by the marriage tie. No human law can abolish the natural and original right of marriage, nor in any way limit the chief and principal purpose of marriage ordained by God's authority from the beginning: 'Increase and multiply'" [RN-12].

- "That right to property, therefore, which has been proved to belong naturally to individual persons, must in like wise belong to a man in his capacity of head of a family; nay, that right is all the stronger in proportion as the human person receives a wider extension in the family group. It is a most sacred law of nature that a father should provide food and all necessaries for those whom he has begotten" [RN-13].

- "On the internal level of every nation, respect for all rights takes on great importance, especially: the right to life at every stage of its existence; the rights of the family, as the basic social community, or 'cell of society'; justice in employment relationships; the rights inherent in the life of the political community as such; the rights based on the transcendent vocation of the human being, beginning with the right of freedom to profess and practice one's own religious belief" [SRS-33].

- "His children, who carry on, so to speak, and continue his personality, should be by him provided with all that is needful to enable them to keep themselves decently from want and misery amid the uncertainties of this mortal life. Now, in no other way can a father effect this except by the ownership of productive property, which he can transmit to his children by inheritance" [RN-13].

- "Paternal authority can be neither abolished nor absorbed by the State; for it has the same source as human life itself. 'The child belongs to the father,' and is, as it were, the continuation of the father's personality; and speaking strictly, the child takes its place in civil society, not of its own right, but in its quality as member of the family in which it is born" [RN-14].

- "The employer is bound to see that the worker has time for his religious duties; that he be not exposed to corrupting influences and dangerous occasions; and that he be not led away to neglect his home and family, or to squander his earnings" [RN-20].

For the Popes, there is no sustainable society, even with abundant resources, unless there is an uncompromised respect for life. "When individuals and communities do not see a rigorous respect for the moral, cultural and spiritual requirements, based on the dignity of the person and on the proper identity of each community, beginning with the family and religious societies, then all the rest—availability of goods, abundance of technical resources applied to daily life, a certain level of material well-being—will prove unsatisfying and in the end contemptible" [SRS-33].

The main issue regarding family, from a business point of view, is to achieve and enable the proper balance of work and family:

more generically, “work-life.” This is even more critical for working mothers. From a Corporate Social Responsibility angle, many of the charters recognize this critical aspect and address the issue with transparency.

I like the definition of work-life that appears in Sony’s Corporate Social Responsibility on-line report: “Work-life balance is the idea that a good balance between one’s occupation and private life can improve both the quality of life and productivity at work. This concept often gathers attention regarding the balance between work and child care due to the accelerating trends of declining birth rate and aging population issues. However, work-life balance also applies to various other areas, including family life or study, and work.”

The economic and social transformations that we are going through since the middle of the last century in developed countries are affecting the ability of families to perform the caring work necessary for the well-being of children that is crucial for sustainable economic development. If we add to this the changes in the demographic pyramid of many of these countries, the end result is a set of imbalances that will have a very serious social impact.

It is in the best interest of companies to come up with changes in the way work is structured to enable a properly balanced work/family ratio. One of the most important methods for this is the use of technology. A simple video conference is enough to eliminate unnecessary business trips that, apart from being an inefficient use of executives’ time, don’t contribute to work-life balance.

I have to admit that one of the major changes I experienced when I moved from Europe to the USA is the amount of additional time that I could dedicate to my family, while at the same time increasing the effectiveness of my work several-fold. The main reasons for this were a more structured workday, and the cultural acceptance and understanding of what constitutes reasonable working hours.

The work-life aspect of CSR is still not widespread throughout the charters that have been published. It is slowly getting through and it is a matter of time before we will see some changes taking place. Probably in this category of CSR there will not be many early adopters and companies will wait to see which models work better. The process will accelerate when companies start losing their talented people to other companies that have a better work-life balance. So far, alternative working schedules, flexible working schedules, work from home, and other strategies are perceived to be very disruptive. As with many other things, sometimes it is just planning and modeling, trying and debugging, that makes any change stick successfully. Sooner or later we will have to figure this one out.

## Human Development—Community

This is an easy element for CSR. It is very pleasing and sometimes easy to donate goods in kind, money, or people time to do something good for the communities we live in. This is very rewarding for the individuals and the companies. In this aspect, there are a lot of similarities between the CSR charters and the social doctrine of the Church; "...then only will true cooperation be possible for a single common good when the constituent parts of society deeply feel themselves members of one great family and children of the same Heavenly Father; nay, that they are one body in Christ, but severally members one of another" [QA-137].

The Popes remind us that some individuals have very important responsibilities towards the community:

- "Rulers should, nevertheless, anxiously safeguard the community and all its members; the community, because the conservation thereof is so emphatically the business of the supreme power, that the safety of the commonwealth is not only the first law, but it is a government's whole reason of existence" [RN-35].

- "The function of the rulers of the State, moreover, is to watch over the community and its parts; but in protecting private individuals in their rights, chief consideration ought to be given to the weak and the poor" [QA-25].

- "[It] is to the interest of the community, as well as of the individual, that peace and good order should be maintained; that all things should be carried on in accordance with God's laws and those of nature; that the discipline of family life should be observed and that religion should be obeyed; that a high standard of morality should prevail, both in public and private life; that justice should be held sacred and that no one should injure another with impunity; that the members of the commonwealth should grow up to man's estate strong and robust, and capable, if need be, of guarding and defending their country" [RN-36].

- "When essential community services are in question, they must in every case be ensured, if necessary by means of appropriate legislation" [LE-20].

- "How greatly such manifold and earnest activity has benefited the community at large is too well known to require Us to dwell upon it. We find therein grounds for most cheering hope in the future, provided always that the associations We have described continue to grow and spread, and are well and wisely administered. The State should watch over these societies of citizens banded together in accordance with their rights, but it should not thrust itself into their peculiar concerns and their organization, for things move and live by the spirit inspiring them, and may be killed by the rough grasp of a hand from without" [RN-55].

- "For the greater man's power becomes, the farther his individual and community responsibility extends.... People are not deterred by the Christian message from building up the world, or impelled to neglect the welfare of their fellows. They are, rather, more stringently bound to do these very things" [LE-25].

- "It should be noted that in today's world, among other rights, the right of economic initiative is often suppressed....It must also be restated that no social group, for example a political party, has the right to usurp the role of sole leader, since this brings about the destruction of the true subjectivity of society and of the individual citizens, as happens in every form of totalitarianism. In this situation the individual and the people become 'objects,' in spite of all declarations to the contrary and verbal assurances...it often happens that a nation is deprived of its subjectivity, that is to say the 'sovereignty' which is its right, in its economic, political-social and in a certain way cultural significance, since in a national community all these dimensions of life are bound together" [SRS-15].

Paul VI and John Paul II offer a new understanding of work as a means of community-building:

- "It is characteristic of work that it first and foremost unites people. In this consists its social power: the power to build a community. In the final analysis, both those who work and those who manage the means of production or who own them must in some way be united in this community" [LE-20].

- “Every effort should be made that the enterprise becomes a community of persons in the dealings, activities and standing of all its members” [PP-28].

- “Each community will be able to set up suitable structures for finding or creating jobs for such people both in the usual public or private enterprises, by offering them ordinary or suitably adapted jobs, and in what are called ‘protected’ enterprises and surroundings” [LE-22].

The main consideration the Popes introduce in this debate is the need for the community to be based on a solid moral foundation in order to be sustainable and deliver progress to all its members:

- “When individuals and communities do not see a rigorous respect for the moral, cultural and spiritual requirements, based on the dignity of the person and on the proper identity of each community, beginning with the family and religious societies, then all the rest—availability of goods, abundance of technical resources applied to daily life, a certain level of material well-being—will prove unsatisfying and in the end contemptible” [SRS-33].

- “Conversion specifically entails a relationship to God, to the sin committed, to its consequences and hence to one’s neighbor, either an individual or a community” [SRS-38].

- “In countries undergoing development no less than in others, the laymen should take up as their own proper task the renewal of the temporal order. If the role of the Hierarchy is to teach and to interpret authentically the norms of morality to be followed in this matter, it belongs to the laymen, without waiting passively for orders and directives, to take the initiative freely and

> to infuse a Christian spirit into the mentality, customs, laws and structures of the community in which they live" [PP-81].

Do companies need to operate morally? I firmly believe that only those companies that are value-driven, and maintain a set of nonnegotiable values that all their members must uphold, can survive long term. Morality confers a sense of purpose that contributes to getting the company focused, and without focus, passion, and determination, companies can't succeed. Long term economic success, eventually, is built on a moral foundation.

## Human Development—The Passion for Excellence

Ronnie Oldham's definition for Excellence is one of the best I have ever read: "Excellence is the result of caring more than others think is wise, risking more than others think is safe, dreaming more than others think is practical, and expecting more than others think is possible. It is the commitment to high-quality performance that produces outstanding results of lasting value. Excellence consists of believing in continuous improvement and never being satisfied with anything being less than it can be. It is quality as a way of life."

It is a never-ending journey. But it has a start. I imagine Excellence as a house with many doors. Every organization has its door to the House of Excellence. Once you find it and bring your team inside, it is very easy to look around and realize that all other aspects of the organization are connected—based on the same vision, sharing the same principles.

"Because order…is unity arising from the harmonious arrangement of many objects, a true, genuine social order demands that the various members of a society be united together by some strong bond. This unifying force is present not only in the producing of goods or the rendering of services—in which the employers and employees of an identical Industry or Profession collaborate jointly—but also in that common good, to achieve which all Industries and Professions together ought, each to the best of its ability, to cooperate amicably. And this unity will be the stronger and more effective, the more faithfully individuals and the Industries and Professions themselves strive to do their work and excel in it" [QA-84].

The relationship among morality, values, and excellence has been discussed by philosophers since ancient times. Aristotelians maintained that being moral is intrinsic to human excellence; Kant thought that human excellence was achieved by living a moral life. At the same time, we previously discussed the meaning of business morality and its connection to company values. So my conclusion is that moral background is the foundation for a set of values that are fulfilled through the pursuit of excellence.

"The norm of human activity is this: that in accord with the divine plan and will, it should harmonize with the genuine good of the human race, and allow people as individuals and as members of society to pursue their total vocation and fulfill it" [LE-26].

## Human Development—Sustainability

Pope Benedict XVI sent this message for Peace Day 2008: "*Per il Santo Padre, la questione ambientale è strettamente connessa con la questione della pace* – For the Holy Father, the environmental question is strongly connected with the concept of peace."

The basic messages derived from the encyclicals regarding sustainability are the following:

- We have the obligation of leaving a legacy of a resource-full world, at peace, for future generations:

"Humanity is advancing along the path of history like the waves of a rising tide encroaching gradually on the shore. We have inherited from past generations, and we have benefited from the work of our contemporaries: for this reason we have obligations towards all, and we cannot refuse to interest ourselves in those who will come after us to enlarge the human family. The reality of human solidarity, which is a benefit for us, also imposes a duty" [PP-17].

- Sustainability has a moral component. We are responsible for the proper use of nature, the renewability of resources, and the consequences of human development: "A true concept of development cannot ignore the use of the elements of nature, the renewability of resources and the consequences of haphazard industrialization—three considerations which alert our consciences to the moral dimension of development" [SRS-34].

- People have the right and the obligation to bring the sustainability agenda forward to become part of the decision-making task of society: "...on the eve of new developments in technological, economic and political conditions which, according to many experts, will influence the world of work and production no less than the industrial revolution of the last century. There are many factors of a general nature: the widespread introduction of automation into many spheres of production, the increase in the cost of energy and raw materials, the growing realization that the heritage of nature is limited and that it is being intolerably polluted, and the emergence on the political scene of peoples who, after centuries of subjection, are demanding their rightful place among the nations and in international decision-making" [LE-1].

# Chapter 9

## *CONCLUSION*

**The Thundering Voice claimed in the desert.**

Paul VI deals with the heart of the problem by declaring that "the economy is at the service of man." What does this mean exactly and how do corporations that have a responsibility to increase shareholder value deal with this fact?

Corporate Social Responsibility is a frame of reference. It is a compendium of all the moral and social obligations borne by corporations—with employees, the communities where they operate, the state that regulates their functioning, their customers who buy and use their products, their suppliers that provide the raw materials and, at the top of the pyramid, the shareholders who provide them with the capital to keep the engine running, and who expect a return on their investment.

Can companies succeed in the long term if they neglect their moral and social responsibilities? Current economic theory says they can't. One single mistake seriously affecting any of the stakeholders and the corporation will likely struggle, and possibly disappear.

What Milton Friedman didn't conclude is that the only way business can escape from the control of governments is by self-regulation, which means that business will consciously develop a set of rules, accepted by all stakeholders, societies, and states, that will bind their actions and meet everybody's expectations for short term results combined with sustainable long term growth. Business has to deal with many states, civilizations, religions, and races in a diverse world. The only way to make everybody happy is to target deep human beliefs and from natural law extract a set of values that are acceptable to all human beings.

On The Carnegie Endowment Web site, Chantal de Jonge Oudraat and PJ Simmons write: "Until recently, most businesses rejected the notion that they had any policy role in global issues, citing their sole accountability to shareholders, profitability and the bottom line. This rationale, mirroring the logic of states that explain actions and priorities based on accountability to their citizens and national interests, was largely accepted. But recently, especially in the 1990s, we have seen a dramatic shift. Citizens, activists, shareholders and governments—particularly in developed countries—are demanding more accountability to those affected by corporate activities. In response, companies have developed and publicized their own codes of conduct, have participated in negotiating industry-wide codes and standards, and have partnered with other companies and non-state actors to pressure other businesses to follow in their footsteps."

Many examples of such narrowly-defined accountability have populated the newspapers for too long and too often. The questions that always come to my mind are: Were the executives of the company, at any time, remorseful of their actions? Did these individuals have a moral frame of reference to understand that what they were doing was wrong? Was the structure of sin so developed that nobody could raise their voice to say that whatever was happening was simply not right?

Corporate Social Responsibility defines the way members of a corporation must behave when conducting business for the corporation; it also provides a moral foundation for social behavior that is expected to be followed by all employees of a corporation at all times. Those behaviors are founded on a set of values that every member of a corporation should live by. Violating those moral and social commandments in or out of the job will result in direct or indirect penalties.

There is not much difference between these statements and the concept of religion. The social doctrine of the Church and the Church's moral and social teachings are a comprehensive foundation for any Corporate Social Responsibility charter. This foundation is actually more complete, cohesive, and congruent than any partially developed set of values and behavioral rules that address only the "flavor of the day" of social concerns.

"Sharing the noblest aspirations of men and suffering when she [the Church] sees them not satisfied, she [the Church] wishes to help them attain their full flowering, and that is why she offers men what she possesses as her characteristic attribute: a global vision of man and of the human race" [PP-13].

Since the first social encyclical, *Rerum Novarum,* from Leo XIII at the end of the nineteenth century, the Church has been shaping the concept of social responsibility. "For toward the close of the nineteenth century, the new kind of economic life that had arisen and the new developments of industry had gone to the point in most countries that human society was clearly becoming divided more and more into two classes. One class, very small in number, was enjoying almost all the advantages which modern inventions so abundantly provided; the other, embracing the huge multitude of working people, oppressed by wretched poverty, was vainly seeking escape from the straits wherein it stood" [QA-3].

International financial institutions also recognize that the only way to make permanent economic improvement in developing countries is to strenuously involve its people, while making sure that the following requirements are met:

- stable political situation

- credible financial institutions
- price stability
- fiscal balance
- trade openness
- special care of the environment

"A 3 to 4 percent GDP growth is insufficient to permit sustained progress on poverty reduction. To overcome this magnitude of poverty and achieve sustainable development, governments must consolidate stabilization; achieve higher and less volatile growth; ensure that growth is environmentally, economically, and socially sustainable; and more effectively involve the poor in the growth process" (The World Bank *Annual Report 1997*).

Human development is at the heart of stable social and economic systems. Corporations that want to grow globally must take this issue very seriously. Governments have to allow this to happen and they need to pay attention to five critical policy areas:

- Improving human and social development;
- Strengthening public finances;
- Reforming and strengthening financial markets;
- Improving legal and regulatory environments to promote private sector activity;
- Reforming the public sector and improving governance.

In the end, it is all about people and the commitment of those individuals, families, and society to develop a set of values that can lay the foundation of stable, sustainable growth.

"Countries that have undertaken serious reform have enjoyed an average two percent higher per capita income growth in the 1990s than those that have not" (The World Bank *Annual Report 1997, Latin America*). That additional growth rate is the difference between real development and never-ending poverty.

When looking at individuals and companies, the same principles apply. Only those companies that have been able to develop a set of values, and especially the "people value," have been able to implement sustainable permanent changes to drive long term performance.

Companies are born out of the vision of a person who identifies a need in society and has the strength and will to put together the critical mass of resources to start up the business and maintain it over time. To make it grow successfully, the company needs to acquire strong organizational capabilities to develop its employees into individuals who are allowed to employ all their knowledge and skills, who know their goals clearly and how they connect to the vision and mission of the organization, with caring leaders that manage wisely and consistently and are not driven only by personal ambition but by their responsibility towards their employees, shareholders and society. "However, local and individual undertakings are no longer enough. The present situation of the world demands concerted action based on a clear vision of all economic, social, cultural, and spiritual aspects" [PP-13].

The social doctrine of the Church has structured a comprehensive message around the following topics:

1. The economy is at the service of man.

2. The integral development of the human person is the key issue to address the social issues of all individuals and communities:

- "The basis for determining the value of human work is not primarily the kind of work being done but the fact that the one who is doing it is a person" [LE-6].

- "When individuals and communities do not see a rigorous respect for the moral, cultural and spiritual requirements, based on the dignity of the person and on the proper identity of each community, beginning with the family and religious societies, then all the rest—availability of goods, abundance of technical resources applied to daily life, a certain level of material well-being—will prove unsatisfying and in the end contemptible" [SRS-33].

- "True development cannot consist in the simple accumulation of wealth and in the greater availability of goods and services, if this is gained at the expense of the development of the masses, and without due consideration for the social, cultural and spiritual dimensions of the human being" [SRS-9].

3. The case for human development is at the heart of Corporate Social Responsibility:

   - "The way to peace lies in the area of development" [PP-83].

   - "For then only will the social economy be rightly established and attain its purposes when all and each are supplied with all the goods that the wealth and resources of nature, technical achievement, and the social organization of economic life can furnish" [QA-75].

   - "However, the picture just given would be incomplete if one failed to add to the 'economic and social indices' of under-development other indices which are equally negative and indeed even more disturbing, beginning with the cultural level. These are illiteracy, the difficulty or impossibility of obtaining higher education, the inability to share in the building of one's own nation, the various forms of exploitation and of economic, social, political and even religious oppression of the individual and his or her rights, discrimination of every type, especially the exceptionally odious form based on difference of race. If some of these scourges are noted with regret in areas of the more developed North, they are undoubtedly more frequent, more lasting and more difficult to root out in the developing and less advanced countries" [SRS-15].

- "The Church has something to say today…about the nature, conditions, requirements and aims of authentic development, and also about the obstacles which stand in its way. In doing so the Church fulfills her mission to evangelize, for she offers her first contribution to the solution of the urgent problem of development when she proclaims the truth about Christ, about herself and about man, applying this truth to a concrete situation" [SRS-41].

4. There is a need for commitment from individuals and corporations toward human development:

    - "It is needed a resolute commitment of each individual—according to the measure of his strength and possibilities—to the struggle against underdevelopment" [PP-75].

    - "Whatever affects the dignity of individuals and peoples, such as authentic development, cannot be reduced to a 'technical' problem. If reduced in this way, development would be emptied of its true content, and this would be an act of betrayal of the individuals and peoples whom development is meant to serve" [SRS-41].

- "It is the responsibility of people of good will to fix the 'social question.'" As Paul VI says: "We are sure that all Christians, our brethren, will wish to expand their common cooperative effort in order to help mankind vanquish selfishness, pride and rivalries, to overcome ambitions and injustices, to open up to all the road to a more human life, where each man will be loved and helped as his brother, as his neighbor. And, still deeply impressed by the memory of Our unforgettable encounter in Bombay with our non-Christian brethren, We invite them anew to work with all their heart and their intelligence towards this goal, that all the children of men may lead a life worthy of the children of God" [PP-82].

- It is the responsibility of the entire world to come together and cooperate. "It cannot, however, be doubted that to attain the purpose we are treating of, not only the Church, but all human agencies, must concur. All who are concerned in the matter should be of one mind and according to their ability act together. It is with this, as with providence that governs the world; the results of causes do not usually take place save where all the causes cooperate" [RN-31].

5. There is a need to establish the right ordering of economic life:

    - "The right ordering of economic life cannot be left to a free competition of forces because rich peoples enjoy rapid growth whereas the poor develop slowly. The imbalance is on the increase: some produce a surplus of foodstuffs, others cruelly lack them and see their exports made uncertain" [QA-88].

- "In order that what remains to be done may be accomplished, and that even more copious and richer benefits may accrue to the family of mankind, two things are especially necessary: reform of institutions and correction of morals" [QA-77].

6. There is a need to have a plan and a structure to succeed:

- "This general analysis, which is religious in nature, can be supplemented by a number of particular considerations to demonstrate that among the actions and attitudes opposed to the will of God, the good of neighbor and the 'structures' created by them, two are very typical: on the one hand, the all-consuming desire for profit, and on the other, the thirst for power, with the intention of imposing one's will upon others. In order to characterize better each of these attitudes, one can add the expression: 'at any price.' In other words, we are faced with the absolutizing of human attitudes with all its possible consequences" [SRS-37].

- "In the first place, it is obvious that not only is wealth concentrated in our times but an immense power and despotic economic dictatorship is consolidated in the hands of a few, who often are not owners but only the trustees and managing directors of invested funds which they administer according to their own arbitrary will and pleasure. This dictatorship is being most forcibly exercised by those who, since they hold the money and completely control it, control credit also and rule the lending of money. Hence they regulate the flow, so to speak, of the life-blood whereby the entire economic system lives, and have so firmly in their grasp the soul, as it were, of economic life that no one can breathe against their will. This concentration of power and might, the characteristic mark, as it were, of contemporary economic life, is the fruit that the unlimited freedom of struggle among competitors has of its own nature produced, and which lets only the strongest survive; and this is often the same as saying, those who fight the most violently, those who give least heed to their conscience" [QA-105].

- The effort has to be planned and executed with distinction. "In order to be fully effective, these efforts ought not to remain scattered or isolated, much less be in competition for reasons of power or prestige: the present situation calls for concerted planning. A planned program is of course better and more effective than occasional aid left to individual goodwill. It presupposes, as We said above, careful study, the selection of ends and the choice of means, as well as a reorganization of efforts to meet the needs of the present and the demands of the foreseeable future. More important, a concerted plan has advantages that go beyond the field of economic growth and social progress; for in addition it gives significance and value to the work undertaken. While shaping the world it sets a higher value on man" [PP-50].

My main conclusion is that to succeed in the long term, Corporate Social Responsibility has to meet the following expectations:

1. *Social Leadership*. Companies must take a leadership position in addressing the issue of Human Development in all its aspects, in an integral way, by investing actively their own free cash to secure sustainable growth for

them and for the individuals they employ and communities they operate in.

2. *Self-Regulation*. Companies have to self-regulate themselves and base their future growth on adding real value to society.

3. *Elimination of Speculation*. Companies have to find a way to expel non-value-adding speculators, financial and non-financial, from the global economic system. Tax burdens should shift from productive activities to non-productive activities.

4. *Sustainability*. Companies have to define the balance between short term profits and long term sustainable growth, paying attention to the responsible use of resources (energy conservation, alternative materials, and waste reduction/reuse/recycling) and the development of sustainable alternative manufacturing and distribution processes.

5. *Tax Solidarity*. Companies should recognize that the economy is at the service of man and not at the service of capital. They should also recognize the social aspect of the taxes they pay and actively ask for the direction of that money toward human development.

6. *Human Development*. CSR models should add a chapter on human development and create an index to measure and compare companies' actions on this subject.

7. *People Value*. People should be the primary value in any business strategy. Values are characterized by the word "always" and companies should always measure their actions based on the final impact on their workers, their families and the communities they operate in, from their suppliers to their customers.

As Dr. J. Robert Ouimet writes in his paper, “Reconciliation of Profits and Human Wellbeing, Is It Too Late?”, “*values that support the singular purpose to multiply goods, create profit and acquire power are not sustainable. It is the obligation of shareholders and management to support a second, more encompassing set of values that recognizes work as a powerful channel to serve people in their material, intellectual, social and spiritual needs. It is possible to foster values that support long-term growth in human happiness and well-being, and also sustain profitability and productivity in any organization. Organizations can create viable, competitive businesses with long-term and high-growth prospects and at the same time, give primacy to human dignity, give meaning to work, and often give a meaning to life.*”

**The End**

# References

[RN] Encyclical *Rerum Novarum*, on the condition of the working people. Pope Leo XIII (5/15/1891)

[QA] Encyclical *Quadragesimo Anno*, on the fortieth anniversary of *RN*. Pope Pius XI (5/15/1931)

Pastoral Constitution *Gaudium et Spes* (Happiness and Hope) on the Church in the modern world. Pope Paul VI (12/7/1965)

[PP] Encyclical *Populorum Progressio*, on the development of peoples. Pope Paul VI (3/27/1967)

[LE] Encyclical *Laborem Exercens*, on human work. Pope John Paul II (9/14/1981)

[SRS] Encyclical *Sollicitudo Rei Socialis*, on the twentieth anniversary of *PP*. Pope John Paul II (12/31/1987)

[CA] Encyclical *Centesimus Annus*, on the centenary of *Rerun Novarum*. Pope John Paul II (5/1/1991)

Thompson, Lindsay J. "Moral Leadership in a Postmodern World." *Journal of Leadership and Organizational Studies*, Vol. 11, Number 1, Summer 2004.

Safty, Adel. "Moral Leadership. Beyond Management and Governance." *Harvard International Review*, Vol. 25, Issue 3, Fall 2003.

# Appendices

## A. The Seven Economic Sins by Pius XI (1931)

- Unquenchable thirst for riches,
- Use of means, fair or foul, to protect their wealth against changes of fortune,
- Buying and selling of goods with the only aim of making quick profits with the least expenditure of work,
- Raise or lower prices rapidly according to their own caprice and greed nullifying the wisest forecast of producers,
- The lack of conscience or accountability of directors,
- Hiding behind corporate name, directors of business companies, forgetful of their trust, betray the rights of those whose savings they have undertaken to administer,
- Crafty men, unconcerned about any honest usefulness of their work, do not scruple to stimulate the baser human desires and, use them for their own profit [QA-132].

## B. The Seven Laws of Social Justice by Leo XIII (1891)

- First law of social justice: Men have the right to own land, means of production and companies.

- Second law of social justice: Men always work harder and more readily when they work on that which belongs to them.

- Third law of social justice: Give men the opportunity to find prosperity in their own land and eradicate the need to migrate if not desired.

- Fourth law of social justice: Men should not be deprived of more than is fair through taxation.

- Fifth law of social justice: Men have the right to have a system that takes care of those much in need.

- Sixth law of social justice: The right to association.

- Seventh law of social justice: The right to have men's religious duties and morality as the most essential component of any social betterment.

## C. The Eleven Laws of Protection for the Working People by Leo XIII (1891)

- First rule: The right to rest on Sunday connected to religious observation.

- Second rule: The right of the worker to be protected from the cruelty of men of greed.

- Third rule: The right to work a reasonable number of hours.

- Fourth rule: The right to rest and break based on job requirement and season.

- Fifth rule: The right of women to have a job according to their strength.

- Sixth rule: The right of children to have a proper developed body and mind before starting their working life.

- Seventh rule: The right to leisure proportional to the wear and tear of his strength.

- Eighth rule: The right to a decent wage to support at least a frugal and well-behaved wage earner.

- Ninth rule: The need to have social agents to regulate and intervene in clear cases of injustice and the role of the state to sanction and protect.

- Tenth rule: The right to earn enough for himself, his wife and children and to save money.

- Eleventh rule: The right to ownership and private property.

## D. The Five Levels of Human Conditions by Paul VI (1967)

- Level 0, Lack of human conditions: the lack of material necessities for those who are without the minimum essential for life, the moral deficiencies of those who are mutilated by selfishness. Oppressive social structures, whether due to the abuses of ownership or to the abuses of power, to the exploitation of workers or to unjust transactions.

- Level 1, Conditions that are more human: the passage from misery towards the possession of necessities, victory over social scourges, the growth of knowledge, the acquisition of culture.

- Level 2, Additional conditions that are more human: increased esteem for the dignity of others, the turning toward the spirit of poverty, cooperation for the common good, the will and desire for peace.

- Level 3, Conditions that are still more human: the acknowledgment by man of supreme values, and of God their source and their finality.

- Level 4, Conditions that, finally and above all, are more human: faith, a gift of God accepted by the good will of man, and unity in the charity of Christ, Who calls us all to share as sons in the life of the living God, the Father of all men.

## E. The Seven Duties of the Wealthy Owner and the Employer by Leo XIII (1891)

- First duty: Not to look upon their work people as their bondsmen, but to respect in every man his dignity as a person ennobled by Christian character. They are reminded that, according to natural reason and Christian philosophy, working for gain is creditable, not shameful, to a man, since it enables him to earn an honorable livelihood.

- Second duty: Not to misuse men as though they were things in the pursuit of gain.

- Third duty: To value them solely for their physical powers—that is truly shameful and inhuman.

- Fourth duty: Justice demands that, in dealing with the working man, religion and the good of his soul must be kept in mind. Hence, the employer is bound to see that the worker has time for his religious duties; that he be not exposed to corrupting influences and dangerous occasions; and that he be not led away to neglect his home and family, or to squander his earnings.

- Fifth duty: The employer must never tax his work people beyond their strength, or employ them in work unsuited to their sex and age.

- Sixth duty: His great and principal duty is to give every one what is just. Doubtless, before deciding whether wages are fair, many things have to be considered; but wealthy owners and all masters of labor should be mindful of this—that to exercise pressure upon the indigent and the destitute for the sake of gain, and to gather one's profit out of the need of another, is condemned by all laws, human and divine. To defraud any one of wages that are his due is a great crime which cries to the avenging anger of Heaven. "Behold, the hire of the laborers…which by fraud has been kept back by you, crieth; and the cry of them hath entered into the ears of the Lord of Sabbath."

- Seventh duty: The rich must religiously refrain from cutting down the workmen's earnings, whether by force, by fraud, or by usurious dealing; and with all the greater reason because the laboring man is, as a rule, weak and unprotected, and because his slender means should in proportion to their scantiness be accounted sacred.

## F. Other Definitions of CSR

There is no universally-accepted definition of CSR. Selected definitions by CSR organizations include:

*Corporate Social Responsibility is the continuing commitment by business to behave ethically and contribute to economic development while improving the quality of life of the workforce and their families as well as of the local community and society at large.*

*—World Business Council for Sustainable Development*

*CSR is about how companies manage the business processes to produce an overall positive impact on society.*

*—Mallen Baker*

*CSR is a company's commitment to operating in an economically, socially and environmentally sustainable manner whilst balancing the interests of diverse stakeholders.*

*—CSR Asia*

*Corporate social responsibility is the commitment of businesses to contribute to sustainable economic development by working with employees, their families, the local community and society at large to improve their lives in ways that are good for business and for development.*

*—International Finance Corporation*

*A concept whereby companies integrate social and environmental concerns in their business operations and in their interaction with their stakeholders on a voluntary basis.*

*—European Commission*

*There is one and only one social responsibility of business—to use its resources and engage in activities designed to increase its profits so long as it stays within the rules of the game, which is to say, engages in open and free competition without deception or fraud.*

*—Milton Friedman*

*Corporate Responsibility is about ensuring that organizations manage their businesses to make a positive impact on society and the environment whilst maximizing value for their shareholders.*

*—Institute of Chartered Accountants in England & Wales*

## G. My Personal Reflections

I think I have to tell you a little bit of my story before trying to give you any advice. I was born the fifth kid of my family in a very depressed area of the very south of Spain. On the south of the south, in a hole, and by the grace of God and my big sister Ana and her husband Pepe, I completed six years of Engineering in 1988. I don't need to bore you with my childhood and other memories. Perhaps you need to know that I learned how to survive and emerge from difficult situations, never losing perspective of who I am, where I came from, what matters, and what my final destination should be. By now, after reading the previous chapters, you might have formed an idea in your mind of what my beliefs are and what matters to me.

I started working when I was fourteen years old. I created my first company when I was still in college and my partners were college professors who I convinced to join me in doing structural design. I certainly learned the subject by working with the best, on real projects. I still can see those buildings now when I go back to Spain, and I feel proud.

My first real job was in France. I moved there one week after Luz and I got married, and we spent six wonderful months in the beautiful Senlis (L'Oise) working in a very high-tech environment that demanded a lot of intellectual power. From there I move to a technology company dealing with engineering systems and very quickly I ended up at Price Waterhouse-Tectel, working on Computer Integrated Manufacturing systems. From there I made the big jump to the automotive industry. My scope of responsibilities brought me into contact with customers all over Europe. I certainly spread my wings in this sector, and I realized what twenty-four/seven service means in a JustInTime environment. I started to understand the people value at a very elementary level. This seed would certainly grow bigger and stronger through the years.

After some years of "fun" and personal development in the automotive sector, I moved to the toy/game sector at Hasbro. My tenure at Hasbro totalled almost thirteen years. I spent the first five years in Spain, dealing with international markets, and in 1999 I moved to the United States with my wife and four daughters. That was a change!

Shortly thereafter I became the Senior Vice President of Operations for Hasbro Games, out of East Longmeadow, Massachusetts. I was thirty-seven years old and I assumed the responsibility of a troublesome facility. The changes that my team and I implemented delivered an incredible performance. The management methodology I used was based on the following principles:

- Management commitment and leadership
- Employee involvement
- Accountability and responsibility
- Gap identification
- Continuous improvement
- When possible, external process certification

There is no doubt in my mind that by declaring and supporting the concept of "employee involvement," I opened the door to an incredible amount of commitment, knowledge, and skills that, in the end, made the difference.

When I decided to leave Hasbro in January of 2006, I spent some months making sure my successor was ready; my main concern was, at all times, to make sure everybody understood how critical it was to sustain the processes we had started with labor's strong support and collaboration.

After some relaxation time, I was very tempted to join Lenox, a division of Newell Rubbermaid. What attracted me was the idea of joining a company that was very successful, a leader that seemed to have a people approach similar to mine and that, with humility, recognized that the company needed to transform itself if it wanted to deliver on its promise to all stakeholders going forward. I brought in my soul with me and it clicked very quickly with the team. I didn't need to reinvent the wheel. My brain was already wired to drive the transformation we needed, one in which we are still immersed.

The economic crisis has brought another dimension to my understanding of social issues. I always remember the hole I came from and I admit I have become more radical in some of my thoughts, in the sense that I need to challenge permanently the adequacy of any action in light of its impact on people and on the community in which I am engaged.

The following 150 thoughts are just very personal ideas that I have developed, learned, or copied through the years and that help me shape my role as business executive. These are the kind of thoughts that can start a great debate about people who really care for other people and their businesses. Enjoy, and don't hesitate to send me your feedback. I am still learning.

## Pedro J. Caceres' 150 personal reflections on business

1. Business success does not happen spontaneously. It requires a clear vision and strategy, a lot of energy, and the right combination of people, process, and technology. It is even more demanding once success has been achieved, to maintain the level of return expected by shareholders, customers, and consumers, and eventually, by the entire society.

2. Successful businesses share common parameters. They are capable of reinventing their business model and adjusting it sooner and faster than the competition, still providing the goods and/or services that consumers are demanding, and maximizing at the same time the contribution along their value chain.

3. The evolution of business management follows universal laws. We could easily model this evolution following Darwin's natural evolution, Newton's classic mechanics, or even with quantum physics and Heisenberg's uncertainty principle. This happens because business has a scientific component that is very important and should not be overlooked. This is the reason why some business models can be taught, learned, and applied in different companies by different people, and if the model is robust and flexible enough, this implementation can be done successfully in all these different companies with predictable results.

4. The real world is full of interconnections of business entities that complement each other in an organized way. Some are producers, and some are distributors, knowledge generators, service providers, technology providers, and so on. The winners know how to combine all these elements to offer a successful proposition to their customers so that both can maximize their business goals.

5. Don't rethink your strategy all the time—implement it. "Land the plane." How long can you wait till you get out of fuel? Ideas? People? Resources? Energy?

6. Your profit goes away through the big gaps of variation around your targets. Close those holes first before you change your targets.

7. Between the black and white, there are many beautiful, satisfactory grey tones: One-Piece manufacturing killed Just In Time.

8. Everything you read in a newspaper can trigger the butterfly effect. In 1992 somebody said that oil should cost $100 and nobody believed him. Read the news every day. What does it mean to you now? And five years from now?

9. Sometimes we think problems are really complicated and we don't even try to go after them. An old king asked his wise men to measure the circumference of the earth. After years of effort, they came back with "approximately 40,000 miles." Then the king asked the following question: "If I wanted to place a rope around the world three feet above the ground, what will be the additional length of rope I need to add to the 40,000 miles?" The answer can be given in seconds—it will be eighteen and a half feet. Now think of your global efforts; how much more rope do you need to add to what you have already done for years?

10. Do you speak more than two languages? If not, you are not global.

11. Global doesn't mean products made in the US and distributed globally. It means made globally and distribute globally.

12. Optimization is the last step in continuous improvement. First, you have to gather all the intelligence about the problem; second, you have to lean issues out; third, you have to gain consistency; then you can start thinking in terms of optimizing.

13. Don't think Six Sigma is just for black belts. Big mistake. Six Sigma tools are to be used, as appropriate and necessary, at all levels of your organization.

14. There is always one door to the house of excellence. Once you go in, look around—everything is related. What is the door to the house of excellence for your company? Is it safety, quality, innovation, customer service…?

15. A production process is like an onion with multiple layers. 1-tool processing material, 2-take-ups and pay-offs, 3-machine housing, 4-interaction machine-operator, 5-process layout, 6-material in-out, 6-warehouses, 7-company distribution and transportation (D&T), 8-customer and suppliers D&T… Only the first layer adds value; the rest is a necessary evil of non-value-added processes.

16. Manage by exception to be an exceptional manager.

17. A perfect manufacturing will never compensate for the flaws of a bad design.

18. Message to the operations people: don't spend your energy second guessing sales and marketing. Understand their goals and give them best cost and flexibility.

19. Remember the Four C's: Commitment, Collaboration, Competence & Contribution.

20. Read selectively and learn how to read quickly.

21. Encourage the rapid transmission of information.

22. Teach people, tolerate their mistakes, and replace them if they are not committed.

23. When thinking of your people, your work is not their work.

24. Sometimes problems are more difficult than you think. And they are always more difficult when they involve people. Do not underestimate the problems that can arise from a mishandled people issue.

25. The five I's for your people: International, Innovative, Integrated, Insightful and Inspirational. You can add Incorruptible if you like.

26. Have passion on execution.

27. The economists say that a low inflation rate is positive because it signals a dynamic economy with pressure for growth and optimal use of resources. I say that a little bit of overtime is positive because it signals that your organization is sized right. Too much overtime means you need to hire; no overtime means you have too many people.

28. Is a plug-and-play organization possible? In the sense of seamless replacements of team members at any level and in any capacity with no disruptions?

29. I needed to create a newsletter to communicate with my employees. I couldn't get anybody to help me, so I learn how to use publishing software. I needed to create a Web site to communicate with all my employees. I couldn't find anybody to help me and I got a certificate in Web design. If you want to do something and you can't find any help, just learn and get it done.

30. People management based on commitment and knowledge: nurture, train, motivate or fire.

31. Progression through training and skills, not seniority. You can establish a loyalty bonus for seniority.

32. What is the probability of nine soldiers moving in the same direction when asked to move randomly without previous instruction? It is almost zero. Sometimes that is what we are asking our teams to do.

33. When the finger points to the moon, some people focus on the finger. This is very painful for any leader if the moon is the destination.

34. My time is spent 50 percent on people, 33 percent on finance, 15 percent on customers and planning, with the remaining 2 percent on technical issues. And I am working in Operations.

35. The dinosaur theory: In everybody's brain there is a little area that contains the learning and instincts from prehistoric times. The dinosaur in every one of us will fight for survival; it will do anything and everything to win in the business jungle. Some have so much fun with these fights that will never be able to create a team; people will follow them because of fear and protection. The T-Rex business leader has no mercy; s/he will eat you up if possible and will show no regrets.

36. Communication: facts, symbols, and emotions. If you don't connect with the sensitive fiber of the people listening, you are not communicating, you are reciting.

37. Do you want to change your organization? First create a sense of urgency.

38. In your first three months, restructure. After one year, restructure again. Get rid of the problems and recognize the solutions.

39. Celebrate anything with your teams all the time.

40. Don't emotionally kidnap your organization. The organization is not there to take care of you and your mood; just the opposite.

41. Align people's self interest to your company's interest. How to do it? That is the fundamental question in business, and it has many answers. There is no silver bullet.

42. Lead by example. Act the way you think or you will end up thinking the way you act.

43. Only in the silence will you hear the answers to your deepest questions.

44. Have personality. Don't copy what others do unless you find it necessary. Your communication plan will be shallow and your people will notice it.

45. Know all your employees' names.

46. Meet all your employees' families. They will be your best retention advocates.

47. Send everybody a card to commemorate events—happy or sad.

48. Manage by thinking about the 95 percent of people who care one way or another, not for the other 5 percent whom sooner or later you will have to fire.

49. There will always be people (5 percent?) who will oppose anything—even a salary increase, overtime, bonus, or time off.

50. Show everyone their "hen." Once upon a time, a film-making crew shot a movie of an African village. When the people living in that village saw the film, they didn't react to it at all. The director was shocked, and asked everybody if they knew what they were watching; one of the villagers answered Yes. She explained that she had recognized her hen running around the village. If your listeners do not see their own "hens" in your picture, they will not engage with you.

51. If you want to have a team, win their souls! Their mind, will, and body are not enough.

52. It is very cold and dark in the top levels of management. To feel warmer, walk the floor of your factory or your office. Talk to the people. They might never understand what you are going through but they care for you. Smell plastic, touch paper or steel, toil with your hands, always with a smile in your face.

53. Your communication program and your training program should be integrated. You are teaching when communicating and you are communicating when teaching.

54. You are as criminal when you rob a bank as when you emotionally kidnap your organization.

55. Labor got organized in the past and gets organized through unions today because of bad, selfish, and/or inconsistent management.

56. From Professor Martinich: "The keys to the production system, however, are the workers in the system. In theory,

all organizations have access to essentially the same standard equipment, materials, and facilities. It is an organization's personnel that provide the competitive advantage and makes one organization more successful than another. It is the people who create new and better products and devise better ways to make and distribute them."

57. Employee ownership: know the goal, vision, mission and objectives. Self-control, gap analysis, corrective action process (Plan-Do-Check-Act). Thriving to master knowledge and skills. Active participant in training, communications, and performance reviews. Seamless behavior transitions in-out of the job. Peer pressure, training, communication, and recognition. Self-motivation to "raise the bar."

58. Differentiate the urgent from the important.

59. Your strategic plan has to be able to fit on one small sheet of paper.

60. Quality is the passion for meeting and exceeding your customers' expectations. If the specifications for your products and services don't help you get there, change them.

61. Mind your own business. Manage your own business.

62. There are two main reasons why projects fail: one, because we don't involve the right stakeholders; and two, because we don't spend time creating and implementing a robust "sustain" procedure. Don't start a project unless you know how you want to sustain it after implementation. You can also add two more reasons: the lack of management commitment and the lack of alignment between goals and expectations and resources.

63. The secret for business success is consistency. Simplify & Standardize.

64. Encourage the rapid implementation of technology.

65. Your business can achieve significant levels of productivity only by intensively using technology.

66. I have seen executives closing down plants and firing a lot of people for selfish, personal career reasons. I have seen them promoted, and eventually, retiring successfully. I asked myself why this can happen. Why don't they find themselves in a situation, sooner or later, as painful as those they create? I never find the answer. I have to remind myself that my actions must be a reflection of my beliefs and I should not pursue personal benefits by making people unnecessarily miserable. I derive pride and joy from letting my teams succeed in the global arena. And if they can't or don't want to, then I am the first to let them go and move on.

67. Strategic vision through a twenty-four-piece puzzle. Ask your team to complete a twenty-four-piece puzzle and it will take them probably less than a minute. Now turn all the pieces upside-down and ask them to do it again. It will take much longer. Why? The answer is that they couldn't see the "big picture"; they didn't have a reference. There was no perceptible relationship between the pieces. This is what we do most of the time with our teams. We don't share information, we don't share results, vision, objectives, etc., yet we want them to complete the puzzle perfectly.

68. What you can't imagine, you can't implement. You have to see and experience a "to-be" situation to be able to get there. If you don't see your moves to "kill the king," don't move a pawn.

69. Do not underestimate the power of a leader.

70. The simplicity of the universe: only three primary colors in the visible world and only seven basic musical notes in Western music are needed to create art. From prehistoric caves to Picasso, from prehistoric chanting to Mozart.

71. The simplicity of the universe: only 103 natural chemical elements, only three molecules bonding, only four forces in the universe (and they might even be expressions of a unified force). And that is what creates life—you, me, and everything else.

72. Why complicate business so much? Simplify: one overarching goal, one vision, one mission, one strategy, one heart.

73. Don't underestimate the power of a vision.

74. To build a company or a capability without regard for the people in the world of which it is a part is a recipe for long term disaster.

75. In this era of constant change, service has become a critical part of a company's offering. Companies not only sell product at a certain price, but also service, and this combination (product + service) is what the customer, and eventually consumers, perceived to form their idea of a brand. Service is delivered throughout the entire commercial effort: product development, manufacturing customized products or packaging, distribution, financial deals, quality inspections, post-sale follow-up, repairs and maintenance, and much more. This sphere of tangibles and intangibles establishes the difference between two different product offerings.

76. Consumer-driven business: the main objective of a company is to satisfy consumer demands through a comprehensive offering of products and services. The consumer is its reason to exist, and has to be part of any critical thinking process. If the company sells through retailers or distributors, it must make sure that it "owns" the consumer in this indirect relationship. It is basically a question of roles and responsibilities in the communication/information chain leading always to the consumer.

77. Innovation: the passion for new products, services, technology, and business processes drives change in the business world. The ability to come up with a different way to satisfy consumer and customer needs, new or existing, is the most elegant and effective way to increase business performance.

78. Competitiveness is the effective utilization of all global resources available to the company to develop its activities. Efficiency is obtained by improving results and/or reducing resources. Competitiveness is improved by enhancing product and service offerings through product cost and service improvements, quality improvement, customer service improvement, expansion of product selection, additional product capabilities, and so on.

79. Business flexibility means being efficiently adaptable to new business conditions, new production volume, new mix, new service-offerings, etc.

80. I detest speculators who don't add any value to the global human system. I admire the hardworking entrepreneurs who risk everything they have to create value and give people and communities a chance to progress.

81. To implement an initiative in a big organization, create a core team of three people for the entire project, define smaller areas, choose one as the pilot area, add three people from each area to the core team and call it the implementation team. When that area is done, move the core team to another area and do the same. You will have consistency.

82. The responsibility of the core team for any project is to define the master plan and master goals, and most importantly, provide consistency to the project as it is implemented in a multitude of areas through the proper creation of processes and procedures, roles and responsibilities, with all of this properly documented.

83. My action plans always have the same format: problem definition, problem description (how much is the opportunity), goals, root cause analysis, contingency actions (what, who, and when), and definitive solutions (what, who, and when). And I follow them up with the same rule: I consider 25 percent completed if the responsibility for the action has been assigned, 50 percent if the solution has been defined, 75 percent if the solution has been implemented, and 100 percent if it has been audited a month later and is still working.

84. Before using business tools, use your intelligence: what do you already know, what can you correlate, what are the real X's (input variables that move the needle in the process).

85. First check if you had a way to make things right, then ask yourself and the team why you did not follow it.

86. Simplify, simplify, simplify again and then optimize.

87. Increase the tempo: plan-do-check-act. Make that wheel turn faster.

88. Not all problems are equal—prioritize! Levels 1-2-3. Give one day to level 1, one week to level 2, and one month for level 3. Do you need to create a level 4, 5, or…? Manage your expectations—you can't be chasing levels 1, 2, or 3 as if they were all level 1, or 10.

89. Don't try to fix variation by aiming for more demanding goals. Fix your variation first and then tighten your expectations and standards.

90. I love Failure Mode and Effect Analysis (FMEA). Tell me what can go wrong and how you plan from the start to prevent it from happening.

91. If you can wait, do not invest until you see that half of your problems have gone away or half of the improvement has been achieved by consistently doing things right. Then invest.

92. Know your financial break-even. Add 20 percent, and make sure you hit it consistently. Otherwise you are dead.

93. To fix an issue, address the process first and then the people.

94. If things are hot, cool them down. If they are cold, heat them up.

95. Teams exist because individuals are extremely limited. We have only a limited amount of knowledge and skill, in a limited range of categories, in a finite time span and finite geographical location. To tackle some problems, we need to work with other people who expand our capabilities.

96. A team needs people who complement one another in: problem identification, analysis, synthesis, implementation, follow-up, and SUSTAIN.

97. A team needs people who complement one another with the following talents: producer, entrepreneur, administrative, teacher.

98. You came to complain to me. Did you try to fix it with your management first? If not, your management is the problem.

99. R&D is pre-production and production is post-R&D. How do you make the integration and transition?

100. Not all products are equal: Mix-Model. Balance the three big operational variables: fill rate, inventory, and efficiency. Find the sweet spot based on a family of products that respond to the same market dynamics.

101. Don't expect tactics that worked once for you will work in every new situation. Adjust as necessary.

102. Base your Continuous Improvement Plan on your top two productivity drivers. Find the levers to transform efforts into quick wins.

103. If you don't plan downtime for the machines, they will plan it for you.

104. A variance of more than 0.05 percent is a crisis (1 percent = 10,000 defective parts per million defects).

105. If you know you have a problem, and you honestly think you have the solution, don't think again—implement it.

106. You can't think and act effectively on more than two issues at a time.

107. Efficiency is a consequence. You have to talk about many issues before you can address an efficiency issue.

108. There is an untapped 20 to 30 percent additional performance capability in any organization. To realize it, you have to align an individual's interests to the company goals.

109. Is it plugged in? I couldn't find the problem with my leaf blower. After one full hour, my five-year-old daughter told me that I should probably plug it into the electrical outlet.

110. It took four years to change a pipe. Every summer I would start up my watering system only to realize that I had a leak in the same pipe as the year before. After three patches, three tubes of glue, a significant amount of Teflon, and many hours of work, I decided to change that one-foot-long piece of pipe and the problem went away. It just took me four years to let go and fix the root cause.

111. The machines feel you. If you are not happy, neither will they be.

112. Contextualize financial results, using comparative or historical data.

113. The law of diminishing returns happens twice as fast as you can predict.

114. When you are growing, all costs and expenses are variable. When you are going down, all costs are fixed!

115. Commit to the core issues and manage by exception.

116. If you are not part of the solution, you are part of the problem.

117. Communicate through 1,001 methods.

118. Ninety-nine point nine percent of people can find any problem for any solution. Only a fraction of those will find a solution to any problem. And a minuscule number of them will consistently find solutions to any problem.

119. Never use percentages, measure in dppm. Make it dramatic.

120. "Eat" your problems—don't send them to your customers.

121. Technical problems have technical solutions. Don't go looking for magic tricks.

122. Everything is about knowledge.

123. At the bottom of my e-mails: "Please consider your environmental responsibility before printing this email."

124. There are some lines that you never have to cross. If you do, you will find yourself in terribly painful situations. There is no way back from some lines. You have to live with the pain for the rest of your life.

125. Do it or don't do it, but don't merely try to do it. –Master Yoda, *Star Wars*

126. Discipline in meditation and in action.

127. Don't trust your memory.

128. Unless you can say "wow" to an idea, don't even try to implement it—it won't work.

129. All business trips are equal, all hotels are equal; all cabs, drivers, meeting rooms, airports, etc., are equal. There is no glamour after your second business trip.

130. First three thoughts when attending a meeting: how to escape safely, who is more attractive, who is not there. The first thought once the meeting is over: what was not said that *you* knew.

131. Never stop acquiring knowledge and skills. Everything is training.

132. If a company is not able to see your value and help you progress as a person and as a professional, it is not your company. Leave.

133. Just talk for one week about a problem with everybody you meet—you will get an improvement of 10-25 percent without investing one dollar.

134. "Let your thoughts be positive for they will become your words, let your words be positive for they will become your actions, let your actions be positive for they will become your values, and let your values be positive for they will become your destiny." –Gandhi

135. If you don't have anyone to talk to about your problems, just talk to yourself. Write your thoughts. Maybe one day you will want to share them with someone.

136. Love your enemies. Hate doesn't let you think straight.

137. Express yourself. You are not insulting by asking for a clarification, expressing honestly your opinion, and proposing an alternative way forward. That is honesty, and your team needs it more than you might think.

138. Experience is a jockey, the horse is knowledge. Experience might let you fix a problem that you have seen before, but it will be only knowledge that will give you the opportunity to satisfactorily address unforeseen new problems.

139. At the end of your days, you will remember only the very few things that really influenced you in life, and they will not be material.

140. I used to be a gladiator who liked to fight, bleed, and win. I had fun crushing my opponents. Now I understand that there is no way you can build a team that way. I still remember how fun it was and I made an effort every day not to do it again. But, my good lord, it was fun.

141. Pray.

142. Do you want to see God face to face? Look in the eyes of a seven-year-old on the outskirts of Mumbai, or Chicago.

143. If an employee comes to you with a problem and no alternatives for its solution and no analysis, send him/her back to rethink the question and start becoming part of the solution.

144. Communication failures? We assume that the following actions are the same: what you say, what they hear, what they understand, what they interpret, what they do. And you are shocked because what they did is not what you told them! I would be amazed if they did it right! And then think of the off-shifts and weekend shifts, and people in remote locations.

145. The path to failure is paved with thousands of good intentions.

146. Your IQ is a useful thing for parties and trivia games. In business it counts for only 50 percent; the other half is your emotional endurance, your solid moral background, your guts, and your courage.

147. Life's key performance indicator: the number of humble, solidary, and merciful reactions to all actions for and against us. The real measure is how we react to anything that comes our way, good or bad.

148. When I felt strong, proud, and powerful, and followed my own instincts, I ended up feeling miserable. When I was humble, solidary, and merciful and following divine providence, I ended up feeling fulfilled.

149. Sometimes unless you touch rock bottom, you can't spring back up. Learn your lesson.

150. Humility is the acknowledgement of the truth. –Father Corapi

**Thanks for reading my book!**

Send your comments to me at:
pedrocaceres@thethunderingvoice.com

LaVergne, TN USA
07 May 2010
181931LV00003B/22/P

9 781608 601349